Loop

LOOP

JOHN TAGGART

Sun & Moon Press
Los Angeles

Sun & Moon Press
A Program of
The Contemporary Arts Educational Project, Inc.
a non-profit corporation
6026 Wilshire Boulevard, Los Angeles, Ca 90036
First published in 1991 by Sun & Moon Press
10 9 8 7 6 5 4 3 2
FIRST EDITION

Some of the poems in this collection have previously appeared in the
following serial publications: *Acts, boundary 2, Box Car, Code of
Signals, Recent Writings in Poetics, Conjunctions, Cream City Review,
Credences, Earlhamite, Epoch, Glitch, Hambone, Ironwood, Jimmy &
Lucy's House of "K," Lana Tack, Multiples, New World Journal, Ninth
Decade* [England], *Northwest Review, Notes, Paideuma, Pequod, Red
Handbook, Red Weather, Sulfur, Syracuse Scholar, Tamarisk, Temblor,
Tyuonyi,* and *Wch Way.*

The author would like to thank the editors of these publications, the
National Endowment for the Arts, the Pennsylvania Council on the
Arts, and Shippensburg University for their support.
This book was made possible, in part, through a grant from the
California Arts Council and contributions to The Contemporary Arts
Educational Project, Inc.

Cover: Edward Weston, *Kelp* 1934
Reprinted by permission from the Center for Creative
Photography, University of Arizona
© 1981 Arizona Board of Regents

LIBRARY OF CONGRESS CATALOGING IN PUBLICATION DATA
John Taggart (1942)
Loop
p. cm
ISBN: 1-55713-012-4
I. Title II. Series.
PS3570, A32L66 1991
811'.54 91-13419
Sun & Moon Classics: 150
Printed in the United States of America

CONTENTS

That This May Be

*Amen: the wish, the desire, that this may be, that
you would give to me and I to you!*
— Olivier Messiaen

As if no one no one were seated beside you no one beside
you as if you were alone yourself completely alone in a
room a room without Ezekiel as if you were completely
alone in a room in a finite room as if no one were seated
beside you when a tongue when a tongue feeds a train when
a violet tongue feeds a violet train into a violet room
when a tongue feeds a train into a room made all violet
in waves of a wide wave on wide wave of a as in father
mist of a thousand waves over you a waves over you alone
among men over you alone when a tongue touches your teeth
in a room made all violet when a tongue feeds a train
into a violet room violet tongue feeds violet train when
a tongue when a tongue feeds a train inside you as if no
one else were seated in a room you alone in a finite room
without Ezekiel as if you were yourself complete no one
you alone as if you alone were yourself complete no one
beside you no one as if no one needed to sit beside you.

Bow your head as son bows only to father.

The train comes through the summer night

violet train through the summer night

it comes in the chopping of a thousands waves

the violet train completely fills a room

in a waves the mist of a thousand waves of a

mist over your head like a light scarf

the train brings a light scarf for you alone.

Bow as son when a tongue touches your teeth
bow to wear a scarf of fire among men
bow as son to be that son and not other.

Sumac

for George Oppen

Freeze-dried, shrunk, crimson
plush crimped, thumbnail proof,
clothed with acid before rain.

One daughter answers beads,
the other flames, anything hot.

Current of pyramids crimson pyramids restless current
in which seeds are thrown syllables of other voices
within this motion as of monuments syllables to awaken
awaken hearts as risen flowers to rise up rise hearts
current of pyramids crimson pyramids restless current.

Current of pyramids crimson pyramids restless current
in which light-entered kings take shoulders for thrones
enthroned like boys riding the shoulders of blind men
drowned kings rise to a new music arise to guide men
current of pyramids crimson pyramids restless current.

Current of pyramids crimson pyramids restless current
in which stars drawn as starfish throng a changeable grid
stars drawn up to beads that return flame-beaded crowns
another answer crowns of love so many crowns of love
current of pyramids crimson pyramids restless current.

O For A Thousand Tongues To Sing

tap & song variations on Charles Wesley

Toom   chicka toom-toom chick—a-toom   .
Toom   chicka toom-toom chick—a-toom   .

No eyes no eyes for the glories for soft moths disks of tinsel
only eyes departed who are words have only eyes for placing
who are only words the departed are only words departed watch
placing don't become confused don't they watch placing of
confidence of foot this isn't real poetry watch foot after *toom*.

T-o-o-m chicak t-o-o-m   t-o-o-m chicak t-o-o-m.
T-o-o-m chicak t-o-o-m   t-o-o-m chicak t-o-o-m.

After *toom* departed watch me watch over my foot watch my foot
that the placing of a foot that my foot not fall not fall on
upturned nail slow motion nail closer and closer in the dream
departed watch that I'm able not because I don't hope able
to turn with the fire wavering fire on the head after *t-o-o-m*.

Tom-chick-tom-tom-chick-tom.
Tom-chick-tom-tom-chick-tom.

Song after *t-o-o-m* I sing the song turning I sing the new song
sing song this could destroy the sense of oneself among things
I sing to departed I remember you Charles Wesley! Charles
Wesley I expand you! words expand words in the hope of fire
saint above watch over who'd sing who'd be turning saint below.

Babble Babble

Ba   ba   ba   ba
     bab   bab   bab   bab
babble   babble   babble   babble

like the solitary child who has no radio who
has no knowledge of how to turn the dial who would not know
how who would not know how constant song is in the air.

Ba   ba   ba   ba
     bab   bab   bab   bab
babble   babble   babble   babble

like the solitary child who has no radio who
has no knowledge of how to move on up a little higher
who would not know how to march all around the altar.

Ba   ba   ba   ba
     bab   bab   bab   bab
babble   babble   babble   babble

like the solitary child who has no radio who
has no knowledge of how it will always be howdy-howdy
howdy-howdy and never good-bye who would not know.

See What Love

Words gather together simple words cold is a simple word
cold a quality of the air the air outside the winter air
winter air as opposed to that of a room the air outside
without the sun a simple word without a thread of the sun
brightness of the air brightness gone is not night fall
night doesn't fall on snow shadows don't snow's snowlit
light grainy light the light simple word light dissolves
grains of light dissolve ruts tractor ruts in the road
song bird by the road not there high song bird not there

children born and left out of doors cannot see the flicker
children left out cannot see the flicker of light shed by
children cannot see the flicker of light shed by bird song

song bird by the road not there high song bird not there
grains of light dissolve ruts tractor ruts in the road
light grainy light the light simple word light dissolves
night doesn't fall on snow shadows don't snow's snowlit
brightness of the air brightness gone is not night fall
without the sun a simple word without a thread of the sun
winter air as opposed to that of a room the air outside
cold a quality of the air the air outside the winter air
words gather together simple words cold is a simple word.

Night falls there is an answer night there night on snow
our lady of dreamed snow won't tell where to build church
light dissolved night falls there is an answer dissolved
bird by road night falls there is an answer night on song
feet of bright angels visit no room angels guard no peace
we lay under bedclothes listening to one another breathe
sun's under no wood sun's under no trees sun's under night
air thick with night the air outside thick with night ash
there is an answer night is an answer night a simple word.

Children born and left out of doors cannot see what love
children left out cannot see what love the father gives
children can't see what love the father gives to his sons.

"See what love   given us
we are called sons   we are."
                cannot be   son outside
of the son   identical

        never be   unless   possess   same
    which the son   has. At present   this is
hidden from us.
                we   understand

Song bird by road see what love there given us not there
grains of light dissolve sons tractor ruts in the road
light grainy light cannot be simple son outside dissolves
night on the son falls shadow identical on snowlit snow
brightness of the air brightness gone is not night fall
without the sun unless simple word possess thread of sun
winter air opposed to the son at present the air outside
cold not hidden from us air the air outside the winter air
words gather together we understand cold is a simple word.

Body And Soul: Poem For Two Readers

take   eat   take   glowing coal   eat

take   coal in mouth   painful

take   pain   pain's privation

                    mouth deprived

take   eat   suffer   lack of

          suffer   lack of fire   coal doesn't

take   fire   take   eat   suffer.

Note: each reader chooses either a left or right page and reads only
those pages. The reading goes from left to right. What is most leftward
on a given line is to be read first. With the exception of the first line
on p. 23, which is the proper beginning of the poem, the lines of both
left and right pages are parallel and, when read together, compose one
single line. Not all spaces are to be spoken in. Also, the sections on
pp. 26-27 are to be read separately. Co-ordination in reading together
may require some practice.

In the face is hidden the original outbreak of all goodness

    no   way   look   into   face completely fire

    so devout so delicate angel eyes   no

    completely fire   completely completely

smiles from bright eyes   bright eyes in vain

    in   vain   life's dreary   for angel eyes

cross heart   hope   hope to die

    no way no eyes look into   love   that   burns

Take   eat   take   eat take   take

take   eat   glowing coal   one for all

take   coal in mouth

                      pain   privation

        naturally   mouth's deprived   mouth's corroded

take   eat   suffer   deprived of

            suffer   "it takes a little time"

take   be soiled with fire

the   face   hide   outbreak   of all goodness

no   way into   face   completely

so   so   angel eyes   no eyes

no way eyes look into   complete   fire

smiles   bright   no

in   vain   no son through tears   none

crossed heart   hope

no eyes   look into love that burns.

heart   lonely,

you   you,   only.

Why haven't you seen it?

    all for you

   spend   days in longing

       you

   all

    believe

   conceive

           the ending

              chance to prove,

  life

You   yours

     surrender

Take heart   take   take   take

                  you   for all

      you   coal in mouth

       all   pain   privation

       days   deprived   corroded

take   eat   deprived of

       suffer   "it takes a little time"

take all   fire

                face   hide   all goodness
    no   conceiving   face   completely
                    so   angel
no way   look into   complete   end fire
smiles'   bright chance
            vain   no son through tears   none
cross out   hope   hope to die
        I surrender dear   to love that burns.

Mild Shouting Poem

Pick a word here are several words
the key to the highway is a word
word's the way to get rid of creatures
there will be time to say your word.

Children in the photograph children ignited
this is not to be considered a miracle
flames running past flame-reflecting signs
they run down the highway run toward you
their enormous mouths speak so slowly
you follow word after word pick one word.

Put yourself in a straight line to your word
word's a flame word a child you are the parent
flame running down the highway runs toward you
no one knows you're the parent except the child
let go your hands to hold out your hands
heart to bones heart to heart burned to bones
resplendent ring of bones sings heart's ease
this is a thought about words pick one word.

Bones sing not distant more solemn sing cordial 50's song
sing in a desert in a desert not in death's dream kingdom

there will be	there'll be time
this is a time	time for you
time to say	say your word
proclaim it	pronounce it

bones not stuffed men bones sing h-h-h-e-v-v-en ah-ha-haa
sing in a desert that's after the highway after the train

another time	time to
follow words	pick one
one word	there's time
mouths speak	so slowly
each speaks	one word
say yours	your word

shining bones sing that's where I want to-oo be-ee-ee-e-e
sing in a desert in a ring a resplendent and opening ring

word's	flame
running	flame
flame	runs
toward	you
you	alone
word	child
you're	parent
pick	one

bones sing in h-h-h-e-v-v-en and parodise oo-ooooo-ooo-oo
sing in a desert sing to let go their hands to clap hands.

Bird Run

Gravel road past "Oasis of Love" parking lot
left at the welding shop follow the tracks
raspberry brambles dull red and chalky white
field not desert where there are no dawn birds
under old Baltimore Road bridge in its shadow
beer bottle necks inner tubes tied at both ends
there are no resplendent bones in its shadow
what do the flowers say to me? say nothing
no violet train vibrates through thinning trees
it's Spring starlings sleeken in the green field.

Very Slow

Very slow from very far away child in slow motion
child not red angel child ignited.

With lilacs the poet would cover death cover with lilacs
he knew death he walked with knowledge and thought of death
bleeding throat song he heard it heard death is lovely
death's soothing serene arrives with cool-enfolding arms
with lilacs the poet would cover death cover with lilacs.

Very slow from very far away child in slow motion
ignited child runs toward you   very slow from
very far away from the horizon in slow motion in
napalm the child runs toward you   over and over
the child begins over and over   very slow from
very far away child in slow motion ignited child
runs toward you   nothing else on the highway
there is nothing else   very slow from very far
away from the horizon in slow motion over and over
ignited child the child in napalm runs toward you.

With lilacs the poet would cover death cover with lilacs
he knew death he walked with knowledge and thought of death
bleeding throat song he heard it heard death is lovely
death's soothing serene arrives with cool-enfolding arms
with lilacs the poet would cover death cover with lilacs.

I would cover death with violet tongue with violet train
tongue feeds train into a room in waves of a as in father
wish desire that this may be mist of the waves over me
mist like a scarf that train might have brought a light scarf
I would cover death with violet tongue with violet train.

Very slow from very far away child in slow motion
a fire-arrow "flaming messages" a child's game
child arrow word on fire running toward you and me.

With lilacs the poet would cover death cover with lilacs
he knew death he walked with knowledge and thought of death
bleeding throat song he heard it heard death is lovely
death's soothing serene arrives with cool-enfolding arms
with lilacs the poet would cover death cover with lilacs.

I would cover death with violet tongue with violet train
tongue feeds train into a room in waves of a as in father
wish desire that this may be mist of the waves over me
mist like a scarf that train might have brought light scarf
I would cover death with violet tongue with violet train.

There will be no cover not the night not even with night
not moody tearful night nor thoughtful shadowy night
not everything can be engulfed in an instant in blackness
death is seeking outstretched hands hands of the parents
there will be no cover not the night not even with night.

Wild Blue Phlox

It was supposed to be outside
labor to cross to not there
to crystal of the wilderness
I've been careless astray also
the wilderness inside within.

So blue is my color after all
distinction of the impoverished
color of movement removement
I am moved to enflamed crystal
my color color of the crystal.

Flower in branched blue flame
flower rendered wild blue flame
flower souvenir of my error
the wilderness inside within
flower how long must we burn?

Brace's Rock, Brace's Cove

for Bradford Graves

And mute he watched till all the East
Was flame: "Ah, who would not here come,
And from dull drowsiness released,
Behold morn's rosy martyrdom!"
                              —Melville, *Clarel*

Flat tide late afternoon the sea a sea of glass
procession the illusion's perfect to the center
child word on fire child on fire napalmed child
there could be procession to the central silence
ourselves to fire-lit crystal of the wilderness.

Scrub like parakeet feathers painted dull ochre
stones to destroy monotony of a plain sand beach
stones and boat the abandoned boat on its side
no one home no painter no poet to pitch stones
beach curves to water c-edged plane of stillness.

Beach to still water c-edged plane of stillness
crippled Lane and Olson and ourselves to center
child word on fire child on fire napalmed child
procession those who cannot wait to the center
we cross through desert of glass to the crystal.

Beach to still water lighted plane of stillness
those who can't wait for veiled reflected light
child word on fire child on fire napalmed child
wilderness light the center wild American light
all into the fire-lit crystal of the wilderness.

All light in fire-lit crystal of the wilderness
light uncirculated all light is from the crystal
dark blue curve to lock crystal on the horizon
dark blue curve of the higher sky a kind of shore
jet vapor clouds along the shore of the visible.

My Name Called Out

My name not behind me not loud it's my name called out
child calls me the same child same child the same word
word and child on fire word and child on fire the same
fire fills the air fire around word fire fills the air
cannot breathe the air I can't breathe no breath given
the air fire-filled air around word air filled by fire
fire the same word and child the same on fire the same
same word same child same calls me word child calls me
it's my name called out not behind me not loud my name.

Answer night fall answer there was an answer
to bird song's flicker of light night on the
flicker the light dissolved where's an answer
to this other light fiery light of word of
the word on fire word and child who calls me
as witness who will help where is an answer to
the word who will help me smother the child?

Cannot breathe the air I can't breathe no breath given
word and child give no breath give none give no choice
none but to smother the child smother the word on fire
embrace word on fire embrace fire to smother the child
smother the child inherit the land inherit desert land
desert in true night true night without pro-dawn birds
without dawn birds without word and child without fire
pro-dawn birds not in the true night not in the desert
inherit desert land inherit the land smother the child
smother child means embrace fire embrace child on fire
word on fire embraced means no one but child smothered
give no choice give no breath word and child give none
no breath given I can't breathe cannot breathe the air.

In the beginning is always the word's always
being born you who will help who expect to be
annihilated who live in expectation of dancing
as bones in the desert you must take and eat
not speak the word let it begin to die in you.

Nativity

If you kneel
sender will teach
will teach you
here's a sender
no bright harness
still a sender
if you kneel
will teach you
teach the shout
sender says listen
listen to sender
sender number one
gle glo glory
that's the shout
if you kneel
sender in white
in greyblue shadows
will teach you.

Sender says listen

gle glo glory

that's the shout

the first shout

listen to sender

kneel and listen

sender number two

no bright harness

kneel down now

sender in lilac

will teach you

bleeding throat shout

the first shout

listen now listen

kneel and listen

sender with fiddle

fiddle without strings

will teach you.

That's the shout

sender number three

in lavender blue

typical heavenly color

will teach you

the first shout

gle glo glory

the bleeding shout

come kneel down

can't you kneel

no bright harness

kneel a little

come listen now

can't you listen

kneel and listen

the first shout

the third sender

will teach you.

From across the sea from across glass
gathered brought together are gathered
as in a mantle as bees in the crystal
gathered brought together by the word
from across the sea cross glass to die.

What glass sea of glass before crystal
who gathered all who hear are gathered
what crystal throne center threshold
what crystal where word is word is stilled
word embraced to die to enter the desert.

Word and child in a blue fire
word and child leap from throne
word and child run toward us.

What word word born unceasingly
what child child calling calling
who're we embracers smotherers.

Wandering no whining boys wandering bones back in the desert
in the desert again the desert with and without possibilities
without harping solemn choir without choir of angel senders
no senders will teach you in true night in true desert night
endless summer night no winter wild for bones away from light
away from the lighted highway from light-reflecting signs
bones play designless play all night long play with all words
play with all the words with the possibility of all the words
all words are possible for bones all for the singing of bones

    how enter the desert with and without possibilities
    how enter the endless summer night no winter wild

cross sea of glass to throne center threshold to the crystal
to crystal where the word where the child is born unceasingly
new-born word and child in blue fire word and child on fire
word and child on fire run toward us calling and calling us
hear the call embrace word and child we are the embracers
we embrace to smother cheek on cheek to smother to make still
still word and child made still cheek made to burn to bones
bones can cross through crystal we can cross to the desert
to all the words to all night long song with all the words.

What pleasure to move among bones in the endless summer night

what pleasure to be capable of motion dance-with-song motion

what pleasure to dance and sing all the words all night long.

Against The Nurses of Experience

The faces of the nurses are green and pale
green and pale faces call to the children
call the children to come home from play
there's no thread not a thread of the sun.

The voices of the children are bone voices
bones sing the song of all possible words
all words all through the night without end
we will never never come in we are at home.

In True Night

1

Of the constant song I keep some of the words
some of the basic words of the song in the air
crystal is a basic word crystal not paradise
procession to the crystal to the child on fire
child the most basic word most haunting word
those who hear cross glass to embrace the child
child embraced to smother not to enter heaven
not heaven but the desert one more basic word
bones basic word enter desert basic word to dance
to dance lily flower dance and forget the steps
to sing the song beyond all songs on the radio.

2

Night falls night fallen true night is fallen
true night truly most destitute time is fallen
destitute most destitute in the midnight hour
it is always the midnight hour in the desert
nothing in the desert to raise the hand against
night falls night fallen true night is fallen
there is nothing no gift to raise the hand for
no love to come no love to come tumbling down
star cannot shine wise men can't find their way
night falls night fallen true night is fallen.

3

Night falls night fallen true night is fallen
true night basic word of the song in the air
crystal basic word crystal in the midnight hour
it is always the crystal hour in the desert
child in the desert child most haunting word
night falls night fallen true night is fallen
nothing there to smother to raise the hand for
no love to come love come one more basic word
bones begin to shine like stars in the dance
lily flower shines wise men can't get the steps
night falls night fallen true night is fallen.

Sine Cura Securum

To lay down in a flame of fire to be in to be at home
in the home land in the region some interior region
interior the land the ground the desert in true night
night after child on fire after crossing through crystal
cross through to join bones in song and dance motion
constant curve of motion safe held safely in the curve
there is safety in the song in the steps of the dance
every step of the dance secure every step without care
song without care every word of the song given weight
word and step given balance balanced in unprotected play
children play without fear of creatures in the desert
in the desert bone children fear no repeated exodus
no repeat for those so gathered no exodus only repose.

I'm talking about love   careless
love   love oh love   hold the
child hold the word on fire   care-
less love   seize keep hold the
child   love oh   careless love.

The Lily Alone

for Susan Howe

Alone lily alone the lily alone looks pantherine
look at the lily at bones as leaves and petals
bones as the ring bones as the ring of the flower
ring of the flower's thought the ring in motion

the motion of the ring is the motion of the animal

skin and muscles burned away the eyes burned also
burned to the essential to bone dance bone song
breath of song like the panther's fragrant breath
listen to the bones they have made your name sweet.

Not Raw Enough

1

Brighten the corner where you are

      Don't wait
      don't wait

until some deed of greatness   don't wait to be lit up
shine   embrace word and child   yes you heard that before
all you hear from me   embrace word and child on fire
shine where you are shine shed your light afar
skies you may help to clear   don't wait to be clear
to be in the ring   ring of bones   not one heart alone.

2

in the cross in the cross

Near   no good to be kept near   try to flag a ride
flag a ride or run   you can run you can run
not to precious fountain healing stream   to be in   in
the cross   don't watch and wait   fire-lit cross of crystal
run to be in the fire in the light of word and child
you can see beyond the river   bones at rest bones at play.

3

day by day his sweet voice soundeth

Daaah dah daaaaah daaaaah
daaah dah daaaaah daaaaah

daaaaah daaaaah daaaaah
daaah dah daaaaah daaah-dah
daaaaah dah dah daaah dah
daaaaaaaah-daah-daah-daaaaaah-daah
daaaaaaaah-daah-daah-daaaaaah-daah

daaah dah daaaaah daaaaah.

4

there's a song in the air

While the beautiful sing   don't you want to hear words
song of all the words in the air   the language song
hear the beautiful bones don't you want to hear all the words
not his sweet voice   wonderful words wonderful words of life
every heart is aflame and the beautiful sing
bones sing all the words   the words sing through the bones.

Twenty One Times

1

Napalm: the word suspended by a thread
the word grows as salt crystallizes
I will grow cells of the word in your mouth.

2

Napalm: leaping as if wrought in the sea
leaping as if pursued by the horse and his rider
a young hart a young heart comes out leaping.

3

Napalm: rub the new-born child with salt
"the fault is that we have no salt"
if the master's word is taken the salt is love.

4

Napalm: soap will not wash the word out
the word breaks through partitions and outer walls
breakthrough of cells of the word in the mouth.

5

Napalm: the heart rubbed and smeared with soap
the young heart is soiled with fire
soap cannot cleanse the soiling of the fire.

6

Napalm: why the child caught on fire
the itching as of creatures for possession of words
glitter for self and nation.

TotalCampus.com Packing Slip

243566937354

Sku	Name	Qty	Price
1557130124	Loop: Poems 1981-1986	1	8.58

TO REORDER YOUR UPS DIRECT THERMAL LABELS:

1. Access our supply ordering web site at **ups.com** or Contact UPS at 800-877-8652.

2. Please refer to Label #02774006 when ordering.

WF

Label #02774006

7

Napalm: the word leaves an acrid taste
the word a thorn in the mouth
the cells of the word connected by thorny sticks.

8

Napalm: edges points of acid edges points of fire
edges and points tear the young heart
tear the heart from doors of the neighborhood.

9

Napalm: the child born again as son of the fire
like and unlike resolved by fire
sunlight on word-hoards dazzling eyes of the nation.

10

Napalm: footsteps ring in a tunnel of the word
tunnel of jacks without a ball
there are four tunnels within each cell of the word.

11

Napalm: ring around the young heart
driven in and driven inward by the hunter's fire
not one door open to the heart.

12

Napalm: child and son wear six corroded rings
no divine light no peace no contentment
no memory no understanding no love for the unloveable.

13

Napalm: a stumbling in chains in the word
a kind of a dance or march not just for ladies' night
footsteps in the dark in the cells of the word.

14

Napalm: fiery chains around the young heart
chain-chain-ch-a—e—a—e—a—e—ain
the heart driven into dark and resonating tunnels.

15

Napalm: if a carpenter's saw cannot be found
if a carpenter cannot be found
child and son must become rings become chains of fire.

16

Napalm: the word lives on like a coal through frost
jelly stays on the mind word in the mouth
cells of the word cells of the burning crystal.

17

Napalm: jellied gasoline turns one thing into another
fool of the fire into heart of the crystal
the young heart becomes the pulse of the crystal.

18

Napalm: it's too late to take the child's hands
it's too late to take the hands of the son into your own
the master says pain is privation.

19

Napalm: the word severed from its thread
the word glows with each breath
I have grown cells of the word in your mouth.

20

Napalm: the glowing crystal records one word
a record of one word plays and plays in your mouth
you will have to know it by heart.

21

Napalm: speak and the word glows and plays
speak and suffer torment for love
because of you no one will have to write the word down.

Through Planes

Grandeur of the house is not the total grandeur
planes of the house planes of a new crystal
a new composition of planes through planes
long ramps lead through planes to the precinct
the precinct without grain boundaries the desert.

Stop upon the threshold or run through the house
the threshold for the caresser of structures
for the fitting of parts for protection of self
or run through the house as if through fire
through planes of fire out into the structureless.

Return To Dehiscence

Earlier, God, man, and the world had appeared reconciled
by the play of the symbolic identity of the three. Wandering
identity, or dehiscence, goes a step further
—Reiner Schürmann

In the end words have been taken away certain no words
taken away to leave gaps as the result of procedure
gaps of no words gaps of silence in a weaver's notation
mystical silence does not replace all the words
words have been taken away to hear and to answer to
hear bones singing high and low singing without effort
answer their song answer that for now is but song's echo.

In the end only bones are left song and dance of bones
the shape of their dance shape of the lily flower
the flower is worthy of love on account of its beauty
little beauty without construction and many imperfections
bones curled around each other as leaves and petals
glimmering of leaves and petals in their dance
only bones standing still in their dance in the desert.

Cloud and fire and the dawn birds have been taken away
pollen people rubbing like snakes have been taken
the burning bush angel is the last to be taken away.

Only bones singing for heart's ease in an opening ring
bone-ring of the bone-flower opening as a sheath of desire
opening *we are the bones of desire* opening
we are the bones of excess opening *the gift which dies.*

There's no releasement into the arms of a loving father
releasement's into the desert without distinction
without sunlight song and dance without ghost shirts.

"Beware"

"Beware" wrote the famous Nicholas of Cusa
and I repeat his word to those who hear
who heard the call of that other word
constant call of that word and child on fire
who heard and smothered the word and child.

Beware of riverbeds into a chemical desert
sediment after rain gully after gully
singing bones won't be found among the gullies
dancing bones won't be found in the shadows
no shadows in true night of the true desert.

Beware of hope the hope of kingdom to come
you are already bones through whom words sing
all the words if one word is smothered
word is smothered if words aren't hoarded
stand against the crows ourselves as crows.

Were You

Notes & A Poem For Michael Palmer

When I began writing some notes for a poetics essay, in response to an invitation from Michael Palmer, there was no thought of turning them into a poem. What happened, however, is that the notes proposed a new poem, one that seemed to satisfy a lack in this collection. You could say the poem meant the demise of the essay. In fact, as I became more involved in the poem's composition, the notes were increasingly taken up with "practical" considerations until they disappeared altogether. The poem ate them up. Perhaps, then, the central principle of any poetics is that it ought to result in poetry. If nothing else, this should moderate the production of poetics essays.

If of interest, the Chernoff book referred to in the notes is *African Rhythm And African Sensibility* (Chicago, 1979) by John Miller Chernoff. The Messiaen poem is my own "That This May Be" (*New World Journal*: Summer, 1980). Caputo is John Caputo, author of *The Mystical Element In Heidegger's Thought* (Ohio, 1978). Spanos is William Spanos, editor of *Boundary 2*; his essay is "The Errant Art of Herman Melville: A Destructive Reading of *Moby Dick*" (unpublished).

—J.T.

12.31.82

Primary: that the presumed goal of community is wrong and probably cannot be attained. The latter because individual vision challenges what has previously existed as a factor (agreed upon image) for unity. Individual vision, when first presented, must be perceived as a threat, actually as something promoting disunity. It's remarkable that Blake continues to act in this way and will no doubt do so into the future. Could a church be organized around Blake?? His vision is too various.

An instance of community is gospel singing. One has to be struck by its power, vibrant out-reaching power and possibility for total involvement. The idea of critical detachment at a gospel service is anomalous. One either joins in or leaves; that's the choice.

The gospel service can't exist without complete prior agreement about the nature of the image/vision and its truthfulness. You can't doubt and sing with abandon. The identification, the location of the singer within the image has to be total. There is no room for the distance of irony.

The poem which establishes community will have to agree, in part, with the language of the old vision. Otherwise, the terms wouldn't be recognizable in any available, present way to an audience.

Am I thinking in terms of too simplistic an opposition in presuming the (new) poem must somehow destroy the old?

This isn't the right question.

There are things to do together and things to do by ourselves.
Projects would be decided by scale. Language is not a project.
By definition, it requires at least two interiors. Is anything
improved when that number is increased? Perhaps the idea of
one speaker and an audience of several auditors only
apparently violates the nature of language as exchange.

Throw out the idea of money. The full house is still attractive.
The larger the audience the more refined in the sense of
simplifying the response. The larger the audience the less the
possibility of involvement of individual members of the
audience unless they confine themselves to the larger, single
wave or direction of single mass response.

If there's to be, ultimately, destruction, then the beginning
must offer the appearance of unified (recognizable) vision.
How this can be done: by a fiction (several people are shown
to sing together), by the use of terms that are evocative of
past visions.

1.2.83

One way to have the poem fail: the audience is encouraged to
be active (outloud) in its response and then is deliberately
confused by the poet. The successful close of the poem is
confusion. The poet has to retire in ignominy (but in secret
triumph).

Poem as gospel service, poem as James Brown.

There should be some statement against performance poetry per se, that—in terms of traditional (tried, actually shared & practiced) ritual, especially by nonironic, non-white groups—it is so trivial, so merely aesthetic. The borrowing of Eno & David Byrne. These should be condemned.

What about the "spirituals" of Coltrane?

Write in the glisses, the sighs, the humming.

Artaud? Important, per Blake, that traditional terms be used. What one wants is such terms with utterly personal (private, untraditional) definitions, e.g., Jesus = the imagination.

There is a place for silence in a poetics. It's the desirable end goal.

Spanos is right to point out Melville's superiority to the Anti-Book, Anti-Scripture, the Satanism of the Romantics. The real test is whether one can stay quiet. Otherwise, each new poem is another mark of failure.

1.5.83

Yesterday, coming back from a walk with Sam, early evening, the sky divided toward the South in zones of color: bottom deep orange with outline of trees; above the orange as it starts to become pale a very light but intense violet; above that the light blue just before nightfall.

Looking back at my notes from Chernoff, I'm reminded that

my assumption that a community, by definition, must be univocal isn't necessary. The community can be a "diversified assembly." The problem is how to make a separate contribution. Should it (can it) stay separate?

1.6.83

That is, separate & together.

first-phrase = (seed of) the patterned = several phrases or sentences; the standard pattern is repeated several times

dance to come out of a trance, to join a diversified assembly with a separate contribution

music & dance: ways of posing structures and restrictions for "ethical actualization"

power of the music lies in silence of the gaps; this is where one's contribution must go & by it the music may be opened up further. The idea is to conceive the music as an arrangement or system of gaps and not as a dense pattern of sound. This rules out Xenakis. What about Riley, Glass, & Reich?

Say the rhythm before you play it. It may not be necessary to express this in nonsense syllables. Perhaps there could be such syllables which coalesce into words as the poem moves along.

1.7.83

Seed pattern: begin with a full phrase or sentence of words, then decompose it to syllables.

New poem should go in collection to break up the finale quality of the two last poems. This one needs to open the conclusion air out, make for a new kind of silence (in, within the poem vs. "stunned" audience). The opening can be combined with the idea of deliberate (designed) failure. Go beyond Eno, that sort of borrowing. James White & the Blacks.

Consider relation of the four parts to gospel song, to the "story" of the broken glass from the signal which means the train won't come on time, may collide with another train, or may not come at all. Forget the red sky, it's too pretty. The opening seed pattern has to be a song of *result*, the state of affairs after the lens has been broken.

Interpolated: put full statements by way of commentary, ie, this is the condition (landscape) that obtains *after* the destruction of the lens. The statements shouldn't be put in a section by themselves, but mixed, perhaps with the nonsense syllables.

I'll free you from demons, not capitalism!

think about it
repeats on the ends of phrases

Take end—work it out, elaborate it (into syllables, becoming
more & more abstract, going toward pure gesture) and then
return to extension of phrase given as words.

Ragged male voice shouting half-phrases, calm female choir
smoothly singing whole phrases or sentences behind him

God has done great things for me (Colossians)
run jump sing & shout

drop piano, organ, bass—expose voices then slowly—fairly
soft—bring them back; end comes on only slightly higher
tone, which is not really close to the intensity of the middle
just before the instruments drop out.

slow, restrained scream

1.8.83

The music is organized to be open to the rhythmic
interpretation anyone present wishes to contribute. This
organization of openness is achieved by the gaps. One makes
one's contribution—a new, additional rhythm—*in* the gaps.

I may be wrong in feeling antagonistic to Peter Gabriel,
reaction of the obscure against the famous. Still, I doubt if the
hybrid is all that desirable. The goal still remains
transformation. It's plagiarism or worse if that doesn't happen.
Not to reproduce a sound, then, but to use it as a general
principle to make another sound.

The train: voice, agent of the voice, the word

1.9.83

train won't deliver burning Dali baby
no Vietnamese doll baby

Opening phrase: talk about the train
time for train talk   a rap??
the student said that just isn't an ordinary train
violet (why violet)   did you expect blue?

rumble of the trains, vibration

the vocal tract (larynx, pharynx, mouth) = resonant chamber

voice organ consists of: power supply
     oscillator
     resonator

The cycle of opening & closing—vocal cords acting like
vibrating lips—feeds a train of air pulses (Beating of the veins)
into the vocal tract. The train of pulses produces a rapidly
oscillating air pressure (throbbing, dilations) in the vocal
tract—a sound.

The sound chopped by the vibrating vocal folds & generated
by the airstream is the voice source. It is the raw material for
speech or song. It is a complex tone composed of a
fundamental frequency & a large number of overtones.

Messiaen identifies mode no. 2 with violet.

Complexes of resonances replace the concept of chords.

1.10.83

& I await the resurrection of the dead?

dehisce   (to yawn)
            to open spontaneously when ripe
            opening of (fruit) capsule by valves, slits, or pores
            splitting into definite parts

einode   das Westgerm
            poverty, want, give oneself away
            jewel   heimat as home (not heaven), homeland

Ezekiel: the voice of the Almighty, the voice of speech
            a voice that was over their heads
            don't fall on your face/no voice

These never unravel their own intricacies, & have no proper
endings; but in imperfect, unanticipated, & disappointing
sequels (as mutilated stumps) hurry to abrupt intermergings—

That profound silence, that only voice of our God...from that
divine thing without a name, those impostor philosophers
pretend somehow to have got an answer; which is absurd, as
though they should say they had got water out of stone; for
how can a man get a Voice out of Silence?

1.11.83

The room (finite, resonant chamber) opens out onto the desert.One side or wall *is* the desert.

pt 1 of poem =a)   train through the summer night, alone in a room, violet tongue (get rid of?), a waves, & Ezekiel (voice & sapphire throne)

           b)   desert   blood dried to dull brown (perhaps have terms of brilliance, but all put in negation, cancelled use   hymn tune

           a)   train

In a system of multi-rhythms—to keep your step—you have to hear the beat that is never sounded (hidden).

rule of repeats   repetition reveals depth of structure (should be more, as *immediate*, in b)

fiction of audience supplying a beat to which I respond, use as basis for elaboration

the gaps: where & how big?
            (never at same place on successive lines)

1.12.83

Looking at the last paintings ('68-70) Rothko did, I'm tempted to stop. Shouldn't the poem—which may be the last one in the collection—be grey, not red or violet?

The gaps in the first section of pt 1 don't seem right. They're at different places on the line, but feel arbitrary. Why should they all be five spaces?

Good rhythm fills a gap in the other rhythms and creates an emptiness that may be similarly filled.

1.13.83

Adapting Chernoff, the open quality of the rhythm becomes a deception; if the call isn't actual, then the response must be strangled. A deceptive call to strangle the response. The organization should *look* open.

So: first pt appears open, to invite response

second is oblivious, completely closed

3rd returns to acknowledge, in terms of 1, that the possibilities are gone (same words, different tone) or that the very same calls are made in this final pt, but they're given without hope. Problem of intonation (on the page).

Re Caputo's comparison (Heidegger & Meister E): an experience with language can lead out, does lead out into "the world."

Term in his letter: *wiederholung*   retrieval of what somehow gets said in the work, not necessarily what its author intended

The difficulty isn't in the cancellation, but in providing something after the x-out. I think this will have to show up in the second pt. This won't alter what comes in the third, i.e., disillusioned repeat or near repeat of pt 1.

perhaps mention the poem is a late thought, something unexpected, added on to the collection

1.14.83

Time to consider what should go in the middle section of ten lines. One thing: it must be continually dense, very tight rhythm.

Think about feeding the Rothko quote (when red does appear, it is like a flame of self-immolation) throughout.

The idea of dried blood as the dominant color, color of the desert.

This is *after* the train doesn't come.

You were waiting alone in a room for the train, in a resonant chamber. One side or wall of the room opens out to the desert. The room, in fact, is more a number of perspective lines than an actual construction of walls.

This section should be so dense that the reader or listener is immobilized, unable to move.

1.15.83

could begin with "were you"

That the section of 10 lines be "about" the closing up of the
gaps, that gaps themselves—with perhaps some quotation
from Chernoff—be a reference.

unresting

Or: leave first part as "fiction"; then the following overlays
operate as commentary (gaps, Chernoff, the revisitation of the
Messiaen poem)

> explanation re lips, tongue
> that the bk. was supposed to be done

Went back to Spanos' essay last night. He argues that
Ishmael, contra Father Mapple, uses language interrogatively.
Presumably this connects with Heidegger's thinking as asking.
He borrows Derrida's process of supplementarity for this as a
process of repetition which always delays a final measuring—
defers presence & thus allows the thing to go on
living. Thus mystery is kept or enacted in an active way as
opposed to the French always mouthing off about mystere, etc.

A naming that's an interrogation of Naming? Does he mean a
questioning of the Word, provenance of His saying? One form
would be to doubt, but not *the doubter* per se, member of a
sect in itself. It seems possible that this is what occurs with
the active use—more than "use"—of metaphor. What separates

it from the New Yorker decorators is that it begins at the beginning of the poem and continues, as a process, throughout. Not merely incidental modification of cast-iron noun structures (always false, whatever the comfort). This may be connected with Ashbery. When I say I want the poem to fail, it's in terms of offering that assuring structure in new & winning ways. Now the interesting thing is to appear to offer just such ways and still make the structure, hope for & claim of structure, fail.

Always erring *words*, not the original/abiding Word

Ishmael has a disaffiliative enterprise

a careful errancy. When Spanos says that seeming for Ishmael is always seeming, the statement affirms the function of active metaphor. This way it's understood that poetry as the formal profession (?) of metaphor will continue—forget the question of audience— because of the nature of metaphor itself (unresting), the end of any single poem or the volume of anyone's collected works no more than a pause, parenthesis that will have to be open-ended on the right-hand side.

per etymology of *Dia-bolos*, poet as scatterer, disseminator, dissimulator—the finite, eccentric, dialogic voice that repeats & retrieves the *dia-spora*

to give undecidability a positive value (negative capability) to bear witness, to be a witness (this doesn't, contra Olson's emphasis on the topological—as if everything happens in terms of space & surface—refer only to object and event.

There *is* the mind, theatre of the mind.

un-name the beasts

tears at his clothes
keep throwing away, speed
up the decay process

1.16.83

Gk ereuthein = to redden

at the least refracted end of the spectrum
color of blood, fire, poppy, rose & ripe fruits

sky at dawn or sunset
of the cheeks, lips
dyed with red   red flag

forget violet

You were

1.17.83

By chance saw the Tarahumara dancers on TV!

1.18.83

Idea for overlay—section 3, over the middle 10 lines—attack
the embrace of the father, embrace of the soul by the father,

at the end of B's Jerusalem. That this—after the picture is given—somehow won't happen, that the Word, contra E, won't be born.

Pulses make sound, and the sound becomes the Word. Perhaps use some of Ong's statements on tbe word as sound.

(For bottom overlay: note that the words—were you ready, etc—are the same, but the tone's changed.)

1.22.83

lines like puffed sleeves

mention the fiction of the broken glass?

This is a dense pattern of sound & not a system of gaps

Melville: imperfect unanticipated disappointing sequels mutilated stumps hurry

Xenakis: a book of screens equals the life of a complex sound

       each screen is made up of cells or clouds of grains

no room inside for movement

Augustine on repetition: a mode of assuring the seeker that he is on his way, and is not merely wandering blindly through the chaos from which all form arises

the train carries & is the voice, is the Word

God speaks his word in the birth of the son

true language = a response to the Word which the Father
addresses
to us (response = letting the Father speak his Word
in us)

all human language must be silenced before the Father speaks

verbum cordis, silent inner word

through song the singer & the listener become identical

Father's son/word is personal & *breath-given*

word is in speaker as seed in source

> the only source of flames
> whose tongue pierces and
> gathers the taste for the
> Word

(last section can deal with the question of whether there's
anything left after the negation)

We don't have the promise of the next breath—Jerry Lee

1.23.83

Gloomy Sunday!

Decided to leave bottom of the first page as it is, a repeat of
the opening. Yesterday I thought it would have to be changed
in the interests of variety. But, as I come to see, this is an eye
demand. When I speak the parts, they're different, i.e., the
opening fairly brisk and aggressive, the close slower and
tentative. The real question is whether there should be, as in
music, reading notation or instructions of some sort included,
put in the margin.

new poem: How To Read Me

section 3 = 13 lines   1 overlap from 2 & 2 lines in the space
between

Ives was trying to protect a fading transcendentalism behind
all the noise, no? *That's* the unanswered question.

1.24.83

What is the connection between the train—train time & being
fed the train—and dancing in the gaps? Turned around, what's
the connection between there being no gaps to dance in and
the train's nonarrival?

In the top & bottom sections, there is the promise of the train
to be fed inside by the tongue of the father. Granted, this is
past tense. (Pages after the first should be in the present?) If

the gaps are closed, there can't be a dance or only a confused attempt. If you can't dance, you can't join the assembly.

First 3 lines deal with the gaps; beginning with the 4th they modulate back to the train or allow some sort of show-through from the middle section.

Perhaps even those lines, the first 3, shouldn't refer to the gaps because the thrust of the second page is clear enough. But: have to keep the last one for the overlap. Their disposition would be completely different if the first of the 3 begins with something other than "if."

Joining the dance =getting on, being part of the train?
Just say no gaps no train.
1st line: carried over from 2 with some addition
2nd & 3rd: transition (gaps —→ train)
4-13: train (use Eck., possibly Ong)

1.26.83

Looks like the whole deal of there being no gaps—or that the gaps have been closed by the song in the air—will have to go in the last section as a series of questions.

2.6.83

"Were You" finished? Happy enough to type it up and clear off the desk of notes and the big cardboard sheets. Final section of 5 lines could go this way:

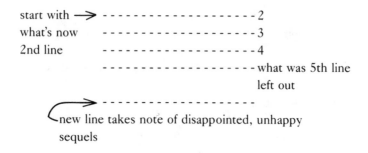

start with ⟶ - - - - - - - - - - - - - - - - - - - 2
what's now   - - - - - - - - - - - - - - - - - - - 3
2nd line   - - - - - - - - - - - - - - - - - - 4
                   - - - - - - - - - - - - - - - - - what was 5th line
                                            left out
         ⟶ - - - - - - - - - - - - - - - - - - -
   new line takes note of disappointed, unhappy
     sequels

But: may be wrong to want more of a da da dum end.
Enough to pause a bit in reading the last line as it is. Let the
past tense do the work. Important that the tone isn't too
harsh; it shouldn't sound superior.

Were You

Were you ready   ready ready   ready for train time
        were you   were you
time to be fed   tongue   to feed train inside you
        were you   were you
train in   in waves of a as in father   amen train
        were you   were you

you were ready you were you were as you were as ready as you were
ready as you could be ready for ready for train time the violet
train you were as ready as ready for the love train "let's start a
love train" you were ready to pull the train ready as could be
to pull the train through the summer night "let's start" ready for
the end of the song "come on come on" ready for violet tongue to
tongue to feed violet train inside train in the train of pulses in
pulses inside you "come on come on" inside you in waves of a
waves of a as in father ready for the end for the father's tongue
you were ready for the father father's tongue to touch your teeth

were you ready   ready ready   ready for train time
        were you   were you
time to be fed   tongue   to feed train inside you
        were you   were you
train in   in waves of a as in father   amen train
        were you   were you.

Were you ready to place your foot in the gaps
were you ready to place confidence in the gaps
were you ready to enter a trance in the gaps.

Were you ready to enter a trance in the gaps were
you ready to do the locomotion in the silent gaps were you
ready to be entranced in the silence in the gaps ready
read-ee-ee-ee you were you were "could be ready for"
you were as ready as rain you were ready to pull
the train through the sum of the song "come on come
to feed violet train insid inside you "come on come o
fa as in father read-ee-ee-ee-ee-ee ready for father
to give the word train of pulses is a word ready to
be fed to be given the inside secret word *verbum cordis*
not say a word hushed to let father let father feed
feed give speak the word hushed in response soul's
language is hushed language of response you were ready.

Were you ready to listen and to understand in the gaps
were you ready to understand with a dance in the gaps
were you ready to do the dip with father in the gaps
were you ready to be embraced like Jerusalem in the gaps
were you ready to give birth to the word in the gaps.

Never Too Late

desan epistamenos, epaoide d' aima kelainon
　　　　　　　　　　　—*Odyssey* XIX, 457

1

One word two vowels one active situation at a time
desan is one word one situation one with two enactors
one situation of tying of binding of tying down
the meaning in vowels enacted meaning in the word meaning

in a long e in eta down in the fair and opened mouth
eta sex queen's vowel fair open mouth the bait
appearance of tits and ass tits and ass appear monstrous
fair mouth sings tea for two you for me ah you for me

in short a in alpha the lowest pitched even rough
alpha = moon = white light = white night-gown
never too late to reread the beautiful mythology of Greece
night-gown twists and twists around you in your sleep

not what was expected not the anticipated enactment
the enactment not anticipated in the situation
combed white heads of the enactors become deathless heads
deathless the dream women who are to be tied down.

2

One word three new vowels another active situation
epistamenos is one word one situation with three enactors
one situation of knowing how to tie dreams down
the meaning in vowels not anticipated in the situation

in short e in epsilon vowel of a new kind of monster
evolution of glitter-eyes the boy-god the thief
new monster sold wisdom for a coat of flames
will trade coat act of the faith that comes with the coat

in short i in iota lips made thin made unclarifying
unclear postcard of sunset skies retouched tinged
iota vowel of the great principle of light vowel of the gilder
would sunlight god decree winter in America wouldn't he

in long o in omega crow vowel crow's caw has an edge
old style monster crow with hooked knife that's crow's bill
supposedly can be imprisoned in winter put him in prison
imprison him fetter him or get ready for combat.

3

One word dipthong two articulations in one syllable
two in one open alpha then glide in direction of iota
there's one active situation under all the others
one situation undercuts others the one situation of dying

aima is one word one situation with me the enactor
do I forget one other word one word before aima
epaoide situation of the new functional charm me the enactor
me to enact the new charm that cuts that opens the wound

bleed is the cry *let it bleed let it bleed's* my cry
the resident power the life the life in common the house
let it let it bleed let it bleed over you all over me
if you need someone to *bleed* on *bleed* all over me

this is the new charm that cuts and opens the wound
new charm cuts new function not the old crow
we've been wounded by phantoms in a wide landscape of snow
cut and open the wound bleed on bleed on the snow.

4

One word vowel dipthong new vowel active situation
kelainon is one word one situation with ourselves enactors
one situation of black of black blood on snow
the meaning in the vowel enacts the meaning in the word

in short o in omicron the vowel of hurt personified
companions of hurt personification of curses
they lead the phantoms back phantoms on the blood-soul
combed white deathless heads new and old monsters

force and motion hunted down in a landscape of snow
this is in black and white this is a motion study
motion almost the same motion almost no motion
the same motion we're the raw heads we're the bloody bones

we are the raw heads connected to the bloody bones
ourselves the enactors of the last word the last situation
not what was expected abrupt night fall on snow
in this night we wander through snow toward the desert.

Orange Berries Dark Green Leaves

Darkened not completely dark let us walk in the darkened field
trees in the field outlined against that which is less dark
under the trees are bushes with orange berries dark green leaves
not poetry's mixing of yellow light blue sky darker than that
darkness of the leaves a modulation of the accumulated darkness
orange of the berries another modulation spreading out toward us
it is like the reverberation of a bell rung three times
like the call of a voice the call of a voice that is not there.

We will not look up how they got their name in a book of names
we will not trace the name's root conjecture its first murmuring
the root of the berries their leaves is succoured by darkness
darkness like a large block of stone hauled on a wooden sled
like stone formed and reformed by a dark sea rolling in turmoil.

Chain Letter

No, I shall not, I will not implore thee
help me, fly to me
here I freeze in the wide, wide world
no sister, no brother, no living thing
that holds me dear. No more   no more
to be an outcast in the world
                    I could tear what I now write
many other sheets, all written for thy eye, but
because in my distraction, I knew not how to write
                    so, behold again how I rave.

      vision   analogous to the narrator's,
relationship with her
      conflict which takes place within
he recognizes the authenticity   of
motionlessness. But
finding a life of   "repose" unattractive
          he   writes
      state of unrelieved despair

I know who implored in the guise of another
I know who wrote the freezing girl's letter
her fatal line in a book no living thing
writer supposed wrote precisely as he pleased
outcast writer the reader of other writers
her line written by him linked to other lines
lines back and forth like links in a chain
caravans in passing charging each other fees
desperate chain desperate readers and writers
I know who wrote know who rewrote the letter
and I know who wanted the chain to be unbroken

Dream not vision dream of passion not vision
not relationship dream in a dream of passion.

I implore your pity for this sin in a dream
enlargement of a desolation lyric bittersweet
not in love enfolded each to each belonging
not both one not one hotly glowing breast
let my letter go unanswered and unrewritten
silence between us silence between us all.

Ceramic From Metepec

Smiling bones with deep red eyes
bones with sticks of dynamite
ribs spines open to the night wind
spine and throat a single trough
you can see the words coming
words of their high and low song
certain words have been taken away
words about the soul's longing
what's left is *wish you were here*.

Repetition

I

This is before the moment of the word
moment of despair moment of the question
there can be moments before that moment
before the word would put out or down
you can be run down by a train of pulses
so step right up step behind the curtain
here's the bride who just can't say no
she'll make you into a poet
every eye's delight every heart's desire
desire is the beginning of this circle.

I'm the bride who just can't say no
I'm the bride who can't help it
can't help it I was born to please
I'm composite the bride of composition
feasible not too strait-laced
I'm the bride of your composition
can't help it I'm in love with you
I'm the bride who's in love with you
I'm the bride who just can't say no.

I'm the bride who just can't say no
I'm the bride who's in love with you
can't help it I'm in love with you
I'm the bride of your composition
feasible not too strait-laced
I'm composite the bride of composition
can't help it I was born to please
I'm the bride who can't help it
I'm the bride who just can't say no.

Who just can't say no I'm the bride
who can't help it I'm the bride
I was born to please can't help it
the bride of composition I'm composite
not too strait-laced feasible
your composition the bride I am
I'm in love with you can't help it
who's in love with you I'm the bride
who just can't say no I'm the bride.

Who just can't say no I'm the bride
who's in love with you I'm the bride
I'm in love with you can't help it
your composition the bride I am
not too strait-laced feasible
the bride of composition I'm composite
I was born to please can't help it
who can't help it I'm the bride
who just can't say no I'm the bride.

II

This circle this circle of repetition
circle opened by disturbance of desire
eye's delight and heart's desire
disturbed eyes and hearts in recollection
recollection is not true repetition
despair of desire despair of the desirer
in despair the question is repeated
will you let father give you the word
will you repeat the word after father.

III

Won't repeat the word won't let father
I won't answer and I wanted I wanted
there comes the question and voices fade
voices of the bride of composition
voices of the bride who can't say no
good to know it's you always miss you
voices from a far border in her voice
images in her unanswering image
unanswering head upon unanswering head.

Unanswering head upon unanswering head
images in her unanswering image
voices from a far border in her voice
good to know it's you always miss you
voices of the bride who can't say no
voices of the bride of composition
there comes the question and voices fade
won't answer and I wanted I wanted
won't repeat the word won't let father.

Won't let father won't repeat the word
I wanted I wanted and answer won't
voices fade and there comes the question
composition bride of voices fades
who couldn't say no bride of voices
always miss you good to know it's you
in her voice voices from a far border
unanswering image in her images
unanswering head upon unanswering head.

Unanswering head upon unanswering head
unanswering image in her images
in her voice voices from a far border
always miss you good to know it's you
who couldn't say no bride of voices
composition bride of voices fades
voices fade and there comes the question
I wanted I wanted and I answer won't
won't let father won't repeat the word.

This is after that moment of the word
moment of despair moment of the question
there can be moments after that moment
after the word would put out or down
you can be run down by a train of pulses
so step right up step behind the curtain.

Pen Vine And Scroll

The intent ear hears the silence hears silence and then the pen
in the silence there are bird calls there is a far away hum
a train could be coming from far away within the silence
the pen scratches and claws making a lonely sound each morning
each morning the silence the bird calls and what could be a train.

Each letter each curve within each letter a vine luxuriant vine
a vine that is made to weave over and under other vines
woven over and under other vines until the letters disappear
the letters are made to disappear in a dark garden of vines
behind the walls of the garden nailed feet and hands peek out.

Scholars are called in to unroll to read and explain the scroll
their eyes blink and shut at the unrolling of the scroll
at the brilliance of the scroll brilliance of marble walls
the scholars are blinded by a brilliance of dark illumination
they are trying to read polished stone or a page that goes blank.

Loop

Arrested for not letting the child be born
not letting the word and child be born
for not letting word and child be born in me.

Detention in my own house with all its stairs
I can look out the kitchen windows of my house
and I can walk up and down the stairs.

Trial in my own room without enough chairs
judge on my chair and jury on the floor
judgement of judge and jury judgement of guilty.

Imprisoned in my own room in my own house
door to my room shut they have shut the door
I cannot look out and I cannot walk up and down.

On the route to releasement in the desert
releasement from the word and child
always I'm always on the route to releasement.

Isolated in my own house with all its stairs
isolation comes after examination
I look out I walk up and down the stairs.

Examination in my room without enough chairs
doctor on my chair students on the floor
diagnosis of doctor a kind of sickness of silence.

Imprisoned in my own room in my own house
door to my room open they have opened the door
will walk with me will walk hand in hand with me.

Let's Be Indians

Let's be Indians on a pilgrimage
pilgrimage up the mountain
Indians in shaggy coats ski-masks
no whistles in the air to begin
no whistles not a sound to the end.

Let's be Indians on a pilgrimage
up the mountain to the glacier
to the field of glacial ice
we cut chunks of the ice
ice that is full of forgetfulness.

Let's be Indians on a pilgrimage
single-file down the mountain
chunks of ice slung on our backs
healing ice for those below
those crying for the suffering lord.

For Jerry Lee Lewis

What's here not what you believe
what's here and not what you believe
not fire that never dies never quenches
bones here and not that fire.

What's here not what you believe
bones here and not what you believe
hell fire that never dies never quenches
me and my bones not fire.

Bones here and not what you believe
not the big black book
black book of burning fire that never dies
bones in slow procession.

Bones here and not what you believed
book of burning fire
bones swerving a little in procession
swerving a little for you.

We are what's here for you Jerry Lee
we're what's here for you
bones and a poet torn in two
me and my bones for you.

Eight Headnotes

for Robert Creeley

I think the central painting is all of one hue: rich, but
muted (as if chalk had been mixed in) violet. There are
great varieties of intensity. But if black has been used,
it was probably first made a grey. The painting has great
density: it looks dyed, saturated. Difficult to tell if
anything like underpainting was used. The range of varia-
tion (light-dark) is very close. Now this painting, be-
cause of the purity of the violet, does shine forth. Its
shining, however, is dusky, almost an indigo.

Patterns in the light-dark contrasts. These strike me as setting up an almost geometric, absolute balance or symmetry. (Idea of marriages performed here/what does a divorce then signify?) The patterns are complex, but I do see a cross. There's clearly a strong horizontal band, about 2' wide, in the upper center; it could have been made with a house painter's brush. This is surrounded by darker wash areas. Interesting that this is made to intersect with strong verticals. The more I look at the central painting the more it appears that Rothko has painted a smaller "Rothko" in the middle of the painting; in turn, this seems part of a larger (subtle) stacking. It's as though two Rothko's were on the same surface. What pushes this idea is the appearance of a spine (vertical) down the middle. (Blaze of sunshine: all the details pick up, but the paintings are too dark to take on any essentially new character.) The spine is not created by painting a vertical stripe (Newman), but by having the edges of the "two" paintings within the painting meet. It's as though each of the two were painted from the far left & far right margins *in*.

The important thing is that the entire painting at the center of the triptych contains several smaller Rothko's within itself and creates, in the process, several cross shapes through the coming together of horizontal and vertical forms. This means that our attention is always engaged, caught, by each portion of the central painting and as a whole. It is, indeed, a center from which there can be "slippage" as the eye travels, but no evasion.

In terms of form, this allows Rothko one more way of filling up such a large space. Stack Rothko blocks on top of one another and fold over the sides (vertical) upon one another and you have a constant cross, crucifixion.

When the child must be weaned, the mother blackens her breast, it would indeed be a shame that the breast should look delicious when the child must not have it. So the child believes that the breast has changed, but the mother is the same, her glance is as loving and tender as ever. Happy the person who had no need of more dreadful expedients for weaning the child!

When the child has grown big and must be weaned, the mother virginally hides her breast, so the child has no more a mother. Happy the child which did not in another way lose its mother.

When the child must be weaned, the mother too is not without sorrow at the thought that she and the child are separated more and more, that the child which first lay under her heart and later reposed upon her breast will be so near to her no more. So they mourn together for the brief period of mourning. Happy the person who has kept the child as near and needed not to sorrow any more!

When the child must be weaned, the mother has stronger food in readiness, lest the child should perish. Happy the person who has stronger food in readiness!

The Rothko Chapel Poem

Red deepened by black red made deep by black
prolation of deep red like stairs of lava
deep red like stairs of lava to gather us in
gather us before the movements are to be made
red stairs lead us lead us to three red rooms
rooms of deep red light red deepened by black
in this first room there is to be a wedding
we are the guests the welcome wedding guests
the groom welcomes us the bride welcomes us
rooms full of deep red light room upon room
in this second room there is to be a wedding
we are the guests the welcome wedding guests
the groom welcomes us the bride welcomes us
the bride and groom take our hands in welcome
room on room third room full of deep red light
in this third room there is to be a wedding
we are the guests the welcome wedding guests
the groom welcomes us the bride welcomes us
bride and groom take our hands in their hands.

Deepened by black red made deep by black
prolation of deep red like cooled lava
the stairs in a cooler prolation of red
there are still the movements to be made
stairs led us led us to three red rooms
rooms of cooled light red cooled by black
in the first room there was a wedding
we were guests we were the wedding guests
groom welcomed us and bride welcomed us
rooms full of cooled light room upon room
in the second room there was a wedding
we were guests we were the wedding guests
groom welcomed us and bride welcomed us
bride and groom took our hands in welcome
room upon room full of cooled red light
in the third room there was a wedding
we were guests we were the wedding guests
groom welcomed us and bride welcomed us
bride and groom took our hands in theirs.

Bride and groom took our hands in theirs
groom welcomed us and bride welcomed us
we were guests we were wedding guests
in the third room there was a wedding
room upon room full of cooled red light
bride and groom took our hands in welcome
groom welcomed us and bride welcomed us
we were guests we were the wedding guests
in the second room there was a wedding
rooms full of cooled light room upon room
groom welcomed us and bride welcomed us
we were guests we were the wedding guests
in the first room there was a wedding
rooms of cooled light red cooled by black
stairs led us led us to three red rooms
there are still the movements to be made
the stairs in a cooler prolation of red
prolation of deep red like cooled lava
deepened by black red made deep by black.

Time for some passion in this language it's time to move
it's time to move to make a move ma—mah—moo-euve-veh
move out of deep red light move out of this purple light
the first movement is the movement of infinite resignation
did you think we would move together move as a gathering
did you think it'd be let's waltz come let's waltz time
it's time to make a move that ma—mah—moo-euve-veh time
move out of this purple light make the move by yourself
first movement of infinite resignation by yourself alone
did you think we'd move as a gathering of wedding guests
did you think it'd be let's waltz like wedding guests time
time for some passion in this language time to move alone
it's time to ma—mah—moo-euve-veh move alone move away
away by yourself away from deep red from this purple light
movement of resignation alone and away from the weddings
did you think we'd move as wedding guests hand in hand
did you think we'd waltz hand in hand with bride and groom
it's that ma—mah—moo-euve-veh time no other move time
always time for that time alone and away from warm welcome
resignation move away from warm welcome of bride and groom
did you think bride and groom wouldn't blacken their hands
did you think their hands wouldn't be as blackened to us
time for some passion time to move into black black rooms.

Time for some passion time to move into black black rooms
did you think their hands wouldn't be as blackened to us
did you think bride and groom wouldn't blacken their hands
resignation move away from warm welcome of bride and groom
always time for that time alone and away from warm welcome
it's that ma—mah—moo-euve-veh time no other move time
did you think we'd waltz hand in hand with bride and groom
did you think we'd move as wedding guests hand in hand
movement of resignation alone and away from the weddings
away by yourself away from deep red from this purple light
it's time to ma—mah—moo-euve-veh move alone move away
time for some passion in this language time to move alone
did you think it'd be let's waltz like wedding guests time
did you think we'd move as a gathering of wedding guests
first movement of infinite resignation by yourself alone
move out of this purple light make the move by yourself
it's time to make a move that ma—mah—moo-euve-veh time
did you think it'd be let's waltz come let's waltz time
did you think we would move together move as a gathering
the first movement is the movement of infinite resignation
move out of deep red light move out of this purple light
it's time to move to make a move ma—mah—moo-euve-veh
time for some passion in this language it's time to move.

Doorway without a door
shadow-crossed doorway
the doorway always open
one at a time inside
inside one hears screams
begins to hear screaming
screams within screams
screams in collision
turbulence of collision
turbulence in the rooms
screams in black rooms.

It is really only one scream
echoes of only one scream in
of one scream within itself
screams within the one scream
within one passionate scream
one scream has been sustained
one scream is being sustained
sustained in one black room
echoes of only one scream in
of one scream within itself
screams within the one scream
the one scream will not decay
not decay in one black room.

Not decay in one black room
the one scream will not decay
screams within the one scream
of one scream within itself
echoes of only one scream in
sustained in one black room
one scream is being sustained
one scream has been sustained
within one passionate scream
screams within the one scream
of one scream within itself
echoes of only one scream in
it is really only one scream.

One scream the motive for movement
movement from one room to another
from one black room into another
into this red room red after black
no red deeper than red after black
one scream the motive for movement
through black through empty rooms
feels like we're wandering through
through a seething and writhing sea
through black through black to red
one scream the motive for movement
movement from one room to another
from one black room into another
into this red room red after black
no red deeper than red after black.

Doorway without a door
shadow-crossed doorway
the doorway always open
one at a time inside
inside one hears screams
begins to hear screaming
screams within screams
screams in collision
turbulence of collision
turbulence in the rooms
screams in black rooms.

Only one scream really it is
only one scream within echoes
itself within the one scream
the one scream within screams
one passionate scream within
been sustained one scream has
being sustained one scream is
in one black room sustained
only one scream within echoes
itself within the one scream
the one scream within screams
will not decay in one scream
in one black room it will not.

In one black room it will not
will not decay in one scream
the one scream within screams
itself within the one scream
only one scream within echoes
in one black room sustained
being sustained one scream is
been sustained one scream has
one passionate scream within
the one scream within screams
itself within the one scream
only one scream within echoes
only one scream really it is.

No red deeper than red after black
into this red room red after black
from one black room into another
movement from one room to another
one scream the motive for movement
through black through black to red
through a seething and writhing sea
feels like we're wandering through
through black through empty rooms
one scream the motive for movement
no red deeper than red after black
into this red room red after black
from one black room into another
movement from one room to another
one scream the motive for movement.

Really only one has been moving us
only one within itself moving us
one scream within itself moving us
screams within the one move us away
away from the weddings wedding rooms
from those to this this black room
to our wandering in this black room
moving in this room means wandering
wandering's moving without meaning
no end to moving in this black room
it is like moving in a writhing sea
we are wandering in a writhing sea
seething and writhing in this room.

Seething and writhing in this room
we are wandering in a writhing sea
it is like moving in a writhing sea
no end to moving in this black room
wandering's moving without meaning
moving in this room means wandering
to our wandering in this black room
from those to this this black room
away from the weddings wedding rooms
screams within the one move us away
one scream within itself moving us
only one within itself moving us
really only one has been moving us.

One scream the motive for wandering movement

movement in one black room in one in another

movement in a writing sea in black rooms

movement into this red room red after black

no red goes deeper than this red after black

one scream the motive for wandering movement

scream from one child who's given one picture

one picture of blood this room full of blood

scream from one child given only one picture

the one child is the poet the child of pain

one scream the motive for wandering movement

movement in one black room in one in another

movement in a writing sea in black rooms

movement into this red room red after black

no red goes deeper than this red after black.

Doorway without a door
the doorway always open
one at a time inside
one at a time I am one
no third person is one
one is I one is I me
the one primitive I me
I me the child of pain
the primitive I inside
inside the turbulence
inside the black rooms.

One I know really one scream
hard not to within one scream
what it is what the movement
same passionate same movement
first movement of resignation
same as before the same alone
away from the weddings alone
not in the wedding pictures
other other possible pictures
blacktop other blacktopped
not in other I me within one
echoes of in one black room
within one in one black room.

Within one in one black room
echoes of in one black room
not in other I me within one
blacktop other blacktopped
other other possible pictures
not in the wedding pictures
away from the weddings alone
same as before the same alone
first movement of resignation
same passionate same movement
what it is what the movement
hard not to within one scream
one I know really one scream.

The motive for movement one scream
from one room to another movement
into another from one black room
red after black into this red room
red after black no red deeper than
the motive for movement one scream
through empty rooms through black
wandering to music played backwards
seething writhing sea through it
through black to red through black
the motive for movement one scream
from one room to another movement
into another from one black room
red after black into this red room
red after black no red deeper than.

Doorway without a door
the doorway always open
one at a time inside
one at a time I am one
no third person is one
one is I one is I me
the one primitive I me
I me the child of pain
the primitive I inside
inside the turbulence
inside the black rooms.

One scream I know really one
one scream within hard not to
what the movement what it is
same movement same passionate
resignation's first movement
the same alone same as before
alone away from the weddings
wedding pictures not in the
possible pictures other other
blacktopped blacktop other
I me within me not in other
in one black room echoes of
in one black room within one.

In one black room within one
in one black room echoes of
I me within me not in other
blacktopped blacktop other
possible pictures other other
wedding pictures not in the
alone away from the weddings
the same alone same as before
resignation's first movement
same movement same passionate
what the movement what it is
one scream within hard not to
one scream I know really one.

Red after black no red deeper than
red after black into this red room
into another from one black room
from one room to another movement
the motive for movement one scream
through black to red through black
seething writhing sea through it
wandering to music played backwards
through empty rooms through black
the motive for movement one scream
red after black no red deeper than
red after black into this red room
into another from one black room
from one room to another movement
the motive for movement one scream.

Been moving me really only one has
moving me only one within itself
moving me one scream within itself
move me away screams within the one
wedding rooms away from the weddings
this black room from those to this
this black room I'm wandering in this
wandering means moving in this room
moving without meaning's wandering
in this black room no end to moving
a writhing sea like moving in a sea
in a writhing sea I am wandering
in this room seething and writhing.

In this room seething and writhing
in a writhing sea I am wandering
a writhing sea like moving in a sea
in this black room no end to moving
moving without meaning's wandering
wandering means moving in this room
this black room I'm wandering in this
this black room from those to this
wedding rooms away from the weddings
move me away screams within the one
moving me one scream within itself
moving me only one within itself
been moving me really only one has.

No red goes deeper than this red after black
movement into this red room red after black
movement in a writhing sea in black rooms
movement in one black room in one in another
one scream the motive for wandering movement
the one child is the poet the child of pain
scream from one child given only one picture
one picture of blood this room full of blood
scream from one child who's given one picture
one scream the motive for wandering movement
no red goes deeper than this red after black
movement into this red room red after black
movement in a writhing sea in black rooms
movement in one black room in one in another
one scream the motive for wandering movement.

It's time to move time for some passion in this language
to make a move ma—mah—moo-euve-veh it's time to move
move out of this purple light move out of deep red light
the second movement is the movement of rosy transparency
move as a gathering did you think we would move together
come let's waltz time did you think it'd be let's waltz
that ma—mah—moo-euve-veh time it's time to make a move
make the move by yourself move out of this purple light
by yourself alone second movement of rosy transparency
as wedding guests did you think we'd move as a gathering
like wedding guests did you think it'd be let's waltz time
time to move alone time for some passion in this language
move alone move away it's time to ma—mah—moo-euve-veh
away from deep red from this purple light away by yourself
alone and away from the weddings movement of transparency
hand in hand did you think we'd move as wedding guests
hand in hand with bride and groom did you think we'd waltz
no other move time it's that ma—mah—moo-euve-veh time
alone and away from warm welcome always time for that time
away from warm welcome of bride and groom transparency move
blacken their hands did you think bride and groom wouldn't
as blackened to us did you think their hands wouldn't be
time to move into black black rooms time for some passion.

Time to move into black black rooms time for some passion
as blackened to us did you think their hands wouldn't be
blacken their hands did you think bride and groom wouldn't
away from warm welcome of bride and groom transparency move
alone and away from warm welcome always time for that time
no other move time it's that ma—mah—moo-euve-veh time
hand in hand with bride and groom did you think we'd waltz
hand in hand did you think we'd move as wedding guests
alone and away from the weddings movement of transparency
away from deep red from this purple light away by yourself
move alone move away it's time to ma—mah—moo-euve-veh
time to move alone time for some passion in this language
like wedding guests did you think it'd be let's waltz time
as wedding guests did you think we'd move as a gathering
by yourself alone second movement of rosy transparency
make the move by yourself move out of this purple light
that ma—mah—moo-euve-veh time it's time to make a move
come let's waltz time did you think it'd be let's waltz
move as a gathering did you think we would move together
the second movement is the movement of rosy transparency
move out of this purple light move out of deep red light
to make a move ma—mah—moo-euve-veh it's time to move
it's time to move time for some passion in this language.

Doorway without a door
the doorway always open
almost the last doorway
one at a time inside
I am one the I me one
a sentence is a choice
I am the child of pain
the primitive I inside
inside the turbulence
almost the last time
inside the black rooms.

Away from the weddings wedding rooms
I have performed the first movement
I have made the movement of resignation
I have moved away all the way away
from those rooms into this black room
this is a different kind of domination
screaming within that will not decay
echoes of one scream within itself
seething and writhing within this room
away from the weddings wedding rooms
from those rooms into this black room
I am not making a move toward ladders
I am wandering again within this room.

I am wandering again within this room
I am not making a move toward ladders
from those rooms into this black room
away from the weddings wedding rooms
seething and writhing within this room
echoes of one scream within itself
screaming within that will not decay
this is a different kind of domination
from those rooms into this black room
I have moved away all the way away
I have made the movement of resignation
I have performed the first movement
away from the weddings wedding rooms.

Red deepened by black red made deep by black
unutterable depth of deep red brought out
what was unutterable brought out in one room
one picture in one room one room full of blood
room where the second movement is to be made
movement of rosy transparency the self rosy
self relating to self willing to be itself
the self itself in this room self transparent
rosy transparency through power of the blood
room where the second movement is to be made
where everything's given everything given back
where the guest enters and welcome is given
bride and groom take hands in warm welcome
the bride and groom take hands in their hands
I am in this room I do not make the movement
don't complete movement I'm the child of pain
I'm the child willing to be that child self
not burning Vietnamese child not Christ child
not rosy not transparent I'm the child of pain.

Doorway without a door
the doorway always open
the last without a door
one at a time outside
I am one the I me one
I don't stop being one
I am the child of pain
the primitive I outside
inside the turbulence
there is no last time
inside the black rooms.

Tourists leave Chapel explosion of their talk
giggles of college girls "could you paint that?"
someone doubts Passion of Christ is the theme
someone dislikes hearing about "blood paintings"
I know a woman who was married in the Chapel
the paintings turned out black in her pictures
blue sky humid afternoon it's Spring in Houston
underneath peeling blue sky I see this red sky
there are swallows darting over a shallow pool
flower beside pool tiny florets like bow ties
ground where the flower grows turns deep red
this ground that keeps turning deep red ground.

Strip Or Ribbon

Strip or ribbon wide ribbon over my eyes
not his eyes not Fuseli's eyes my eyes
not one glance of involuntary revelation
of the room and of the second movement.

Another strip or ribbon wide ribbon over my lips
not his lips Fuseli's blackened halloween lips
not one glancing word of involuntary revelation
of the room and of the second movement to be made
the strips or ribbons wide ribbons made of words
worn and frayed words against getting carried away
doorways washed in blood doorways to the room
where bride and groom take hands in their hands
the strips or ribbons wide ribbons made of words
against being carried through doorways in blood
child of pain's words against power of the blood
not Vietnamese child not Christ I'm the child
this is a kind of silence a poet's kind of silence.

Rule 14L

1

An audible voice to third power read power to the third power
the voice more powerful than the striking of chimes or bells
the voice through fences and hedges even the blue mountains
read power to the third power read power projection of power
more than chimes or bells the voice the throwing of the voice
even blue mountains the voice straight through every surface
read power projection of power read process read power process
the throwing of the voice eating of the voice the voice eating
through every surface through every face out there in radioland.

2

Read process read power process everything is going smoothly
the voice eating every face despite the rolling of the eyes
every face out there in radioland every face seized and eaten
everything is going smoothly the voice's teeth find every face
despite the rolling of the eyes despite sticking out tongues
every face seized and eaten every face squealing as it's eaten
the voice's teeth every face teeth eating instead of laughing
despite sticking out tongues eaten turned to stinking darkness
every face squealing as it's turned into the train of the voice.

3

Approaching public crossings at grade prolonged or repeated
to be prolonged or to be repeated until crossing is reached
approaching locations where men may be at work on the tracks.

4

Eating instead of laughing there is the question of survival
turned to stinking darkness in cars that can't be disconnected
turned into the train of the voice the real mystery train
there is the question of survival question of keeping a secret
in cars that can't be disconnected to fall down in the cars
the train of the voice the real mystery train the slow crowd
question of keeping a secret a secret face that stays secret
to fall down in the cars to fall down to play dead in the cars
mystery train the slow crowd that can have no disconnection.

Monk

1

A-bide   a-   a-
bide

    fast falls
    the   tide

    fast

the darkness deepens

2

with   abide

with

When others   fail

             fail

             fail

comforts flee

fail   flee

3

abide with me
abide with me

me   me

Three

A closed space may hold many turnings
neither ciel nor Jerusalem to be found
turning after turning away from the goal
path and only path turning after turning
the goal is neither ciel nor Jerusalem
what's found turnings in a closed space
many turnings the route is undiscovered.

A cloud may or may not contain grains
the rectangles of a cloud may be empty
empty rectangles no grains of sound
better to have a very high mean density
rectangles in which disorder is perfect
high mean density almost a white sound.

A fence may be made by a form of words
the field fenced all the tables fenced
a form of words that cannot be opened
held together by a tension of attention
tusk cannot open it flower cannot open it.

Not Quite Parallel Lines

1

One end of the column in pencil larger than the other
out of the larger emerges still another column
actually two columns in pencil emerge from the first
the conjoined columns graphs of pitch against time
the first is held out held like an arm in blessing
the second column descends widens as it descends
end of the second is wide and the beginning of third
the third is a column of fire with hissing points

two lines two not quite parallel lines in extension
if the two lines were colored they would be colored red

sequence of the film follows sequence of the music
the poem is a sequence from graphs of pitch against time
in the film I'm arrested for not letting the child be born
sequence I can look out the kitchen windows of my house
the judgement of judge and jury judgement of guilty
sequence I cannot look out and I cannot walk up and down
they'll walk with me they will walk hand in hand with me
diagnosis of the doctor is a kind of sickness of silence
sequence in isolation in my own house with all its stairs
always it seems I'm always on the route to releasement.

2

Sound backwards sound can be made to pass backwards
made to pass backwards to its source by graphs
begin with extinction of sound and end with the attack
the attack is a diamond shape that becomes an arrow

by definition the arrow belongs to the class of weapons
fragments have been found throughout the country
the fragments mean that it has always been with us
has always been with us the arrow that flieth by day

it can enter the air with a minimum of resistance
edge opened only a slit then a resounding tearing

the searching for an edge and then the tearing
this is the constant humdrum constant humdrum of life

a present with its point intact and gift-wrapped
Sam & Dave: "wrap it up/I'll take it" always taking it
impossible in fact to carry on business without it
but something no one in his right mind would dwell on.

3

The waves spread out and out from one source of power
the question is where will you and I position ourselves
there is the source of power and there is the wave
the waves spread out to become one standing wave
one standing wave from one source which is the horn
the one wave which is a kind of arrow a kind of weapon

to look directly down into the mouth of the horn
who would not think twice about calling it "my" horn
into the power supply the oscillator the resonator
like peeping to secrets through a strange bird's eyes
this is where the growl and the shout come from
the horn is the instrument of the growl and the shout
who would have dreamed the horn must be opposed
I must oppose the horn by deformation of association

back to the wave and to the question of position
the wave may become a blade broad as the horizon itself
or it may become narrow with a sharp point wrapped in fire
whether horizon or wrapped point the question remains

agreed oh what a beautiful morning is one position
the moon faint crescent still out and high up in the sky.

4

These tongues of fire from the mouth of the horn
who knows what tongues sound like sound like hissing
pity for those who lie out on the tongues
mercy pity peace and love consumed by the tongues of fire

the flexed arm has little need of a hammer
there is more than sufficient power in the arm
arm that is that arm that is arm and horn of power
arm and horn not held like an arm in blessing after all

two lines again two not quite parallel lines again
they are like the opened mouth seen from the side
an abstraction or schematic of the opened mouth
it also could be said to be on its way to possibility

dump truck from Selmer delivers its load of glow
its load pours out in not quite parallel lines
faithful from the One Mind Temple position themselves
the faithful position themselves "to feel the glow"

repeated cries of warning from those who lie out
what are their cries in comparison with the tongues
what can their cries do against the class of weapons
their shrill cries can do nothing against glowing weapons

the red tongues fully extended from the opened mouth
body of the tongues and tip of the tongues extended
the tongues neither Dionysius' nor a dinosaur's
tongues of the typhonian voice letting them all hang out.

Uncovered Vine's seen by the rifled sepulcher of kings
he is one of the funeral men who puzzle and tease
one who would withhold the key even from friends
it may be the cross-purposes of life make one shy
make for a quiet man who won't be touched by argument
how know such a man "except in shadow from the wing"

heir to funeral man throwing stones at his shadow
the one who is throwing stones at his own shadow
and to the other one neither one a euphonist of academe
the other one who speaks to fill trying pauses
the one whose supplement is life in boats and tents
one the other I am heir to these exceptional natures

and to two other funeral men who are two black men
two black men who are "blues people" two horn players
one experienced an awakening during the year 1957
was revealed to one he had the right seal in his forehead

the horn is the instrument of the growl and the shout
and if and if the horn what of the scratching pen
who would have dreamed that there must be opposition
heir to and opponent of these exceptional natures.

Bell of the horn the bell or mouth directly overhead
naked men upside-down naked men play overhead
world in flames typifies the end and the beginning
skeleton heads smiling into the mouth of the horn

the hand strikes against the hand at obtuse angles
glancing blows hand against hand like cymbals
hands entranced in the gaps in between the beats
hand against hand bleeding hands bone against bone

I looked at the lily at bones as leaves and petals
ring of the flower ring of the flower's thought
now the motion is different turned into slow motion
ring now excrement of the voice slow train of excrement

perhaps nothing more than the stereotypical chase scene
special effects adult language some violence
see this horn drives people crazy then it eats their
call a spade a spade then it eats their faces away

two lines again two not quite parallel lines again
lines of the opened mouth the class of weapons
wavy lines wavy glowing lines pulling the disco crowd in
the glowing lines from an old tune "Blessed Assurance."

The player is breathed through completely and gently
through so completely so gently he hardly feels it
the player of the horn which drives people crazy
the player feels elation and elegance and exaltation
people put hands in put their whole selves in the gaps
what the people feel is their faces being eaten away
the player experienced an awakening during the year 1957
the player is not a perturbation of the voice's breath

I've been arrested for not letting the child be born
been arrested for not letting the child be born in me
for not letting the word and child be born in me
word and child another kind of instrument of the voice

two lines again two not quite parallel lines again
of the opened mouth the class of weapons word and child

paint and ink on vellum a page from the Apocalypse
the horn is sounded followed by hissing hail and fire
hissing hail and fire mingled with blood on the earth
the player's erect not a fold of his garments disturbed.

8

The horn sounded summons sounded and a raggedy march
summons and a march and suddenly crying and whimpering
growl from the back of the throat rough R&B growl
shout from the back of the throat rough R&B shout
the growl and shout recorded live June 14, 1964
and whimpering bloody heads running out in the night

it was revealed to him that he had the right seal
the player is not a perturbation of the voice's breath

use a stack of amps use another another and another
turn them up turn them up to get a wall of sound
turn them all up until your ears are washed in blood
turn them up and still not close to the voice's breath

the player thought your strength was in your blood
bloody head blood down your face not close to the voice

paint and ink on vellum a page from the Apocalypse
the horn is sounded burning mountain cast into the sea
hissing as the burning mountain is cast into the sea
the player's erect not a fold of his garments disturbed.

Come down to one word who would've dreamed one word
this one terrible word even this doesn't mean the end
there can be opposition by deformation of one word
there can be opposition to the humming of one word
I like to write something that people can't hum
that people can't hum can't put entranced hands in
people can't put entranced hands together in the gaps
can't put their whole entranced selves in the gaps
one end of the column is larger than the other
the end of the second is wide and beginning of third
I am twisting these conjoined columns of the horn
deforming the horn trying to deform the horn of the voice.

The Reading of Something Written (1)

to bring
one thing beside another

bringing together into lying before

The gathering of the vintage
Picking and gleaning
the fruit

that snatches things up
the conclusion

If we are blind
the collecting follows the picking and gleaning, the
shelter follows the collecting

To be one to be one thing beside another
one thing beside another to be gathered
remain one thing one thing beside another
to be brought together to lie before
to lie before to be part of the gleaning
part of the gleaning part of the gathering
part of the gathering part of the picking
to be one thing be something the fruit
to be one thing something brought together.

That that snatches things up is the voice
snatches up beginning of the conclusion
something brought together kept safe
brought together kept safe for the voice
if we are blind we are the stinking fruit.

To be part of the gathering the conclusion
the collecting which brings to conclusion
which brings to and which is governed by
that conclusion the voice's conclusion.

Part of the collecting picking and gleaning
stench of what follows the final collecting.

The Reading of Something Written (2)

We are all ears

                invasion of sound

                    the sound of a word

               We have heard

    this is nothing else than   letting

        It lay one   It lays one

                          This

          comes to pass

       without qualification

To be invaded by sound interiors invaded
invaded by the sound of word and child
having to hear the voice through a speaker
having been invaded having to hear the voice
having been invaded having to go on hearing.

Ourselves letting ourselves nothing less
ourselves letting ourselves be gathered
gathered by word and child for the voice
the voice lays one the voice lays another
lays one interior lays another the same
letting ourselves lie together before
letting and lying gathered by a speaker
hearing occurs in us because of a speaker
hearing in us has to be a kind of mishearing.

To have heard the speaking word and child
ourselves lying together because of it.

By virtue of having to hear there is the lay
ourselves lying together before the voice
this comes to pass without qualification
the lay comes to pass if we do not mishear.

The Reading of Something Written (3)

There is only

the question of what

The Lay

laid

whatever lingers awhile

collected and brought forward

before and down into

it discloses what is present

what is present

whatever remains

To be part of the answer to the question
only the question of what the lay laid
no need for Heraclitus to tell us the answer
to be part of the answer from the beginning
part of everything present for the lay.

What is present is disclosed by the voice
to have to be what's present in concealment.

To be part of everything present to be laid
to believe to be laid is to be sheltered
that whatever lingers will be sheltered
whatever lingers is collected brought before
is collected and brought before the voice
before and down into the train of the voice
has to endure in the low cars of the train
disclosed as part of the stinking darkness
disclosure in the train the stinking darkness.

Before and down into the train of the voice
to be part of what is deposited in the cars
there must be a concealing from revealing
reservoir of concealment not to be drawn from.

The Reading of Something Written (4)

the Lay

always means

language

the essence of language

Nothing less than

the essence of language

sound   voice

To be gathered means gathered to be laid
gathered by the word and child to be laid
word and child play the procurer's song
to be gathered means to be laid by language.

Nothing less than to be laid by language
the essence of language the voice that lays.

To be laid by language the voice that lays
what was present in lying together before
to have dwelt in the lying together before
to have dwelt be dwelling in the low cars
in the low cars that's where we're dwelling
the essence of language the voice that lays
that lays and deposits us in the low cars
analysis of what has come to pass by noses
what can be done against what's done to us.

Part of the answer to the question of what
answer in the low cars where we're dwelling
essence of language the voice that lays
sound of the voice re-sounded but crookedly
tongue of the voice must be crookedly embraced.

Antimasque For Antonio

1

What you want I've got it what you need is a face
no face and it's no dice rolled in no silence.

2

An actor to remain silent what you need is a face
word-face to remain silent in a space made of words.

3

Teeth all white skin brushed and without blemish
5x7 photograph hand-tinted for the sake of appearance.

4

Not a tinted photograph what you need is a face
I've got it word-face for the sake of disappearance.

5

An actor can be made to undergo gradual disappearance
curtain on curtain transparent curtain on curtain.

6

Yet I'm child of pain I have no transparent words
no transparent words what's left word of resignation.

7

One word of resignation not transparent resigned
resignation to move away in a space made of "despaire."

8

Move alone and move away move away from their wedding
not what you wanted not this kind of disappearance.

9

What I've got not what you wanted word of resignation
your face word-face one-word-face of resignation.

10

Not what you wanted not this kind of silence
no dalliance no smearing the bride's wedding gown.

In Itself

The line exemplifies, embodies; it is in itself metaphor.
—Robert Duncan

In itself it is in itself that the line is metaphor
in repetition in the repetition within the line
repetition is choice each repetition a choice rechosen
constant repetition in the line a constant choosing
what is chosen is the metaphor image of the metaphor.

Image of the metaphor image product of metaphor process
product of metaphor process and product of the line
Zukofsky: "it ought to be involved in the cadence"
what is to be seen involved in what is to be heard
what heard what seen what I choose to hear and to see.

What's seen what's chosen is the image of the voice
the image breaks through closed spaces clouds and fences
I had thought these forms of words could not be opened
image in the line breaks through paw of an animal
image of the voice what I hear what I'm chosen to see.

Prayer No. 20

To be out in the world to be language-less
to be out in the world without language
protected as in a house from language
not to be misled by the security of a house
as if the danger and terror were far away
the danger of being willing to be in pain
terror of being laid by the voice that lays.

Lab Notes

These are stripped-down versions of notes for a presentation
given at the George Oppen Conference sponsored by the Archive
For New Poetry, University of California–San Diego. Their title
comes from Ted Pearson. The entries under 4.7.86 are all quota-
tions from George Oppen's letters to myself. Those under 4.8.86
are all quotations from Martin Heidegger's essay "What Are Poets
For?"

4.3.86

Why is the speech of the poem to be more valued than other
speech? Because it's involved with a greater density of
figuration, metaphor, and thus—perhaps—vision. Common-
place that "poetic language" vs. ordinary discourse resists
being used up in action. There is the desire to state a
vision, to maintain that vision, and to have it acknowledged,
if not admired, by others. *Need* more to the point, need—and
obsession?

A church is a house built on vision, vision acted on and or-
ganized around. Why this is to be avoided: the church, like
any structure or system, wishes to maintain itself. Vision
frozen. One certified vision and one certified way to read it.

How to keep vision from being turned into a church (if not a
conference): keep it moving, in motion.

To keep your voice from being appropriated, turned into an organizing principle: it must move and change, perhaps be displeasing or somehow confusing, unrecognizable; above all, it must move.

4.4.86

One way is silence, gaps of space left between parts of the line and other lines. Silence as white space or as the production of the disjunction of syntax. Curious that the sense of movement comes from having to bridge the gaps, supply the verbs. Sense of movement almost consciousness itself.

Paradox: the voice retains motion and a kind of definition-in-motion by means of silence, the introduction of syntactic awkwardness, disjuncture. This *could* turn out to be simply the more convolute expression of the riddle; a measure of technical skill, cleverness, a delay before we're returned to absolute orthodoxy.

Acoustically: the voice is articulate on the page because the edge of silence is always present, let "into" the poem.

4.5.86

Back to the first question. Why should I, or anyone, wish or
be expected always to speak as a poet? Does it have little to
do with poetry and mostly with a conception of self, a role?
Sounds like a half-baked *Psychology Today* number.

And at my back I hear—Marvin Gaye!

The poet undergoes a kind of martyrdom by sticking to one
voice. This has to be judged as deliberate, conscious, be-
cause what allows you to become a poet in the first place is
attraction to, ability to reproduce other voices, other "rou-
tines" in writing. Being a young poet amounts to trying on all
the various voices.

To be a poet, you have to hear the voices, be able to write in
a variety of voices. Some never escape their "ability."

So, the intricacies: to be able to hear and reproduce other
voices, yet not be captured by them. Then to choose to stay with
one voice, denying in effect that which made the poetry possible
in the first place.

Monk. Naturally, there were the charges that he couldn't play.
Mary Lou Williams remembered when he had a lot more
technique.

Why anyone should deliberately lose technique. Ethical, ethics.
A choice made on the basis that one voice, one body of technique
is somehow truer than others. The "verification principle" here

is vision. You make the choice because of vision. And the vision is singular. Difficult to deny the feeling it chooses you instead of the other way around.

4.6.86

Our attention is drawn toward or by a quality of aware sacrifice, aware restriction. Distinction between the intelligent and otherwise admirable artist who makes appropriate use of available technique — even bothers to study — and the poet of vision.

Why vision can be repellent to those so apparently intelligent. Objection of the informed that it isn't up to date. Underlying all their objections, animating them, what throws current agreed upon taste into question, if not outright denial: the spirit world (& disregard for bantering irony, which is a protection against that world).

Vision is the big picture. "Phemenological."

4.7.86

the poem is the moving edge

Therefore consciousness in itself, of itself, carries the principle of *actual ness*. This is indeed the law and the prophets. Perhaps this should have been the meaning of objectivism

"Objective: objectivism"
That even sorrow or the most terrible would may prove one to be part of the universe, not excluded, not fallen from it. There is no other sincerity

This is the definition of 'objects'

4.8.86

...these more venturesome ones must dare the venture with language.
The more venturesome dare the saying.

...in what direction is that to be said which the sayers must
say? Their saying concerns the inner recalling conversion of con-
sciousness which turns our unshieldedness into the invisible of
the world inner space.

...those who are more venturesome cannot be those who merely say.
The saying of the more venturesome must really venture to *say*.
The more venturesome are the ones they are only when they are
sayers to a greater degree.

4.9.86

The "poet's question": when is there song that sings essentially?

But our interest has to be all the other way: subversion of any such essential song. And here we are, friends, back to silence. When is there silent song?

Tempting to consider that poetry, manifesting vision, makes for destitution. Snapshot or radiant rose, the poem presents what hadn't been there before. What a reader's made aware of is the lack of this in the world. The poem makes the reader destitute. Art povera in the result or effect of the poem rather than in the poem itself? Perhaps poetry has been responsible for "romance," hunger for a time or condition that never was. Could there be such a hunger without poetry? No Hesiod, no gods? *Contra* only a god can save us, only silent song.

When we turn from the poem, what we have to feel is the falling away, the utter lack of its clarity all around us. Perversion of all "realist" art.

4.10.86

Not to get caught up in the complications of argument. If not
the question, one of the questions: how is speaking as a poet
different from anyone else's speaking or being spoken by
language?

I've written it's a matter of vision. But if we are spoken
through, bespoken, by-words or adverbs of the saying of language,
then isn't the vision hopelessly controlled from the beginning?
We say/see what the play of the saying of language
allows us to say/see.

To ask if anything can be done presumes there's something un-
desirable about a human person defined as a "loudspeaker."
There is! Simply wilful pride? Avoidance or rebellion against
the speaking, however, has my sympathy. Antonio, surly and
avaricious as he is.

To work for vision, valuing it beyond all else. And, instead of
the mystical rose, to come up with a dark world dominated by a
ruthless, indifferent sea on which we must have our precarious
existence. "How wild the planet is." Or: the voice that will
eat your face away.

Can anything be done? Vision, what's to be *opposed*. To speak as
a poet is to speak according to a vision *and* to speak in contra-
diction of vision as it's given by language insofar as the
speaking or calling of language would make the poet no more
than a passive "transducer."

214

Speaking as a poet means finding a way to let silence into our speaking, to speak and yet be silent. "Speak, without words, speaking, to speak and yet be silent. "Speak, without words, such words that none can tell."

Marvin Gaye Suite

1

17 seconds of party formulaics by professional football players
intro of 17 seconds of hey man what's happening and right on
party of those gathered to be laid by the voice that lays
don't have to be a jock to be gathered brought together for the lay
Marvin mixed over the party Marvin calls out twice to mother
surely mother must be the answer forget about the father's tongue
if not one then the other not father unexpected relief of the other
mother blackens her breast mother goes to bed with father
Marvin left with the father Marvin calls three times to father
Marvin calls father father father we don't need to escalate
Marvin calls out three times to father within the father's house
isn't this ironic you probably can't help but feel superior
calling out three times to father in the house of the father's voice
listening to Marvin I want to cry it makes me want to cry
like Edgar witnessing the maddened king arraigning his daughters
isn't this ironic calling to father in the father's house
another call can he get a witness somebody somewhere
and in the mean time it's right on baby it's right on right on
I'm a witness I'll talk to him so I can see what's going on
what's going on party of those gathered brought together for the lay
party of those gathered to be laid by the voice that lays
those who believe that to linger and tarry is to be sheltered
I'll talk to Marvin I'll talk to you who have yet to be brought together
what's going on what's always going on in the house of the voice.

2

Bass figure fat half note two eighths another two and hold
"I'd attribute the Motown sound to Jamie Jamerson's busy bass"
sound there before Motown sound of the voice busy before the bass
Marvin wants to know what's happening the voice is what is
the busy voice is what's happening what is happening across this land
Marvin wants to know what else's new cause he's slightly behind
nothing else what is what's happening the voice is what's happening
Jamerson died of complications from a heart attack in Los Angeles
Marvin stopped "Sexual Healing" show to pray for his soul
Marvin stopped asking for that sexy rhythm for that sexy beat
"and the beat was largely the invention of Jamie Jamerson"
the voice busy before the bass the beat the voice's invention
to pray is to stop asking to pray is to be silent to remain silent
silent remain silent until the voice is heard the voice of the father
isn't this ironic you probably can't help but feel superior
isn't this ironic to stop asking for that rhythm for that beat
to stop asking be silent until sound of the father's voice is heard
the busy voice is what's happening what is happening across this land
would it do any good to pray for Marvin who doesn't understand
would it do any good to pray do any good to pray for Marvin's soul
I'm a witness wandering witness not praying I'm wandering
wandering means moving with the wrong rhythm on the wrong beat
listening to Marvin I want to cry it makes me want to cry
I'm a witness I'm wandering not praying wandering on the wrong beat.

It's not doo it's who Marvin taught how to fix his mouth muscles
it's who-who-who Marvin taught to make his breath part of the sound
his breath part of the phrasing his breath part of the sound
the sound there before Marvin the sound of the voice busy before Marvin
it's not who-who-who it's *oooooo—oooooo—oooooo* it's a hook
it's a hook made smooth made so very smooth *oooooo—oooooo—oooooo*
the singer has been hooked so very smooth that he hardly feels it
so smooth *oooooo—oooooo—oooooo* so smooth he hardly feels it
what the singer feels is elation and elegance and exultation
he's part of the sound part of the sound of the voice
what the singer feels is a high he's flying high in the friendly sky
Marvin thought cocaine was the boy who made slaves out of men
it's not cocaine it's the word and child who fixed Marvin's mouth
so smooth *oooooo—oooooo—oooooo* so smooth he hardly feels it
the singer feels he's flying rest of the folks lay their bodies down
party of those gathered to be laid by the voice that lays
hooked and gathered by the voice through Marvin's voice to be laid
those gathered feel their faces being eaten away they don't care
been hooked so very smooth the folks want to linger they want to tarry
hook made smooth made so very smooth *oooooo—oooooo—oooooo*
you can think you won't be hooked by the hook of the father's voice
you can think you won't be hooked by the hook of the singer's voice
Marvin thought cocaine was the boy who made slaves out of men
you can think you won't be hooked by the voice through Marvin's voice.

I just want to ask about world in despair world destined to die
what would that be would be without hope would be that world
without hope of kingdom to come without the river of water of life
river of water of life clear as crystal proceeding out of the throne
children held in the crystal river thread of remembrance severed
world without hope of kingdom to come that would be that world
that the river would dry up it would river dried-up riverbed
Marvin asks who really cares who's willing to try to save a world
he means world of hope of kingdom to come he means this river world
isn't this ironic asking to save this world that will not die
this world of hope of kingdom to come father's world that won't die
Marvin wants to save this world for the children let's save the children
let's save the children (spoken) let's save all the children (spoken)
save the babies (sung) quick fill on soprano save the babies (sung)
"perhaps the single most emotional moment he ever reached on record"
Marvin used multitracking to sing with himself speaking and singing
his singing voice higher than his speaking almost a woman's voice
speaking and singing the sound of the voice through his voice
I just want to ask a question what we're saving all the children for
what we're saving all the children for saving them to be laid
this is the father's world this world won't die father's voice won't
saving the children to be gathered together in this world of hope
children in river of water of life proceeding out of the throne
children in the crystal river the thread of remembrance severed.

Downshift from dig it everybody to think about it to talk about it
three times from Marvin don't go and talk about my father
the warning given three times don't go and talk about my father
three times the warning given in a voice made smooth so very smooth
don't want to don't want to and have to have to talk about father
I'll tell you I'm a witness I'll tell you what's going on
what's going on party of those gathered brought together for the lay
gathered by father's voice through Marvin's voice to be laid
one reason Marvin loved father was because he offered him Jesus
Marvin was thrilled and fascinated with the idea of tarrying
that's where you wait where you repeat over and over
over and over thank you Jesus repeat over and over thank you Jesus
where you repeat over and over thank you Jesus for minutes and hours
repetition is choice you choose to be part of the party that waits
those who believe that to linger and tarry is to be sheltered
Vaughan the Silurist warns of the deliberate search for idle words
of the leaving of *parricides* behind and no other monument
as if there needed to be another as if any other monument were needed
this is the father's world it won't die father's voice won't
don't want to don't want to and have to have to talk about father
Marvin was shot twice by his father on April 1, 1984 in Los Angeles
Marvin was shot twice by his father in his father's house
yes if you linger and tarry you will be sheltered in his house
in his house are many mansions in his house there are many parties.

6

Shared term between last song and this song the term is mercy
when you call on him for mercy father he'll be merciful my friend
Marvin knows when you call on him he'll be merciful
when you call there's response it's that old call and response
call and response of the father's voice sound of the father's voice
"sound unites groups of living beings as nothing else does"
united gathered by the sound of the father's voice through Marvin
groups parties of those gathered brought together for the lay
house full of people from which no one as of yet has gone out
people in the house of the father's voice father's voice won't die
where did all the blue skies go is a question they can answer
went into the house the blue skies went into the father's house
the blue skies went into the father's house mercy mercy me the ecology
people call for mercy and there's the sound of the father's voice
blue skies call and there's the smooth and zealous sound
call and response of the father's voice sound of the father's voice
sound unites groups of those who were living as nothing else
ah things are what they used to be ah what they used to and ever will be
same as they ever were give Mr. Byrne some credit same as they were
there has got to be a way Mr. Byrne's burning down the house
Pointer Sisters are burning they're burning doing the neutron dance
the house won't burn the father's house won't burn down to the ground
Marvin's in the house Marvin knows when you call on him for mercy
call and response of the father's voice sound of the father's voice.

6

Oh feel it feel it oh everybody feel it Marvin knows that's alright
he knows that's alright people oh when we're loved by the father
the father knows that's alright Marvin knows that's alright
everybody feel it at the love party of those gathered brought together
those gathered by the voice through Marvin's voice to be laid
sound of Marvin's voice good to party fun to party with you baby
sound of Marvin's voice the thrill is real and it's oh so good baby
Marvin pronounces "thrill" so that it rhymes with "real"
Marvin was thrilled and fascinated with the idea of tarrying
over and over thank you Jesus until you feel your face being eaten away
feel it feel it everybody the thrill is real and it's oh so good baby
Marvin feels there's only time for praying and for a love party
to pray is to stop asking is to be silent to remain silent
Marvin sings the lord's prayer on his 'Dream of a Lifetime' album
the singer has been hooked so very smooth that he hardly feels it
those gathered feel the thrill of the father's tongue against their teeth
if you let him Marvin will take you to live where love is king
Marvin will take you where love is king the king and his secret life
love four times in a row love four times so smooth and so zealous
listening to Marvin I want to cry it makes me want to cry
like Edgar crying through his babble song *I smell the blood*
isn't this ironic you probably can't help but feel superior
there has got to be a way and there is no way out of the house
I'm a witness wandering not praying wandering in the house of the voice.

Holy to be wholly holy is to be wholly the excrement of the voice
the excrement the stinking fruit the stinking darkness in the low cars
to be wholly holy is to be in the low cars in the train of the voice
come together people got to get together to be wholly holy
you've got to believe whatever lingers and tarries is sheltered
there can be a train in the house there can be many trains in the house
you can pull the train at the love party of those gathered together
those gathered by the voice through Marvin's voice to be laid
sound of Marvin's voice good to party fun to party with you baby
you can pull the love train baby right on honey right on
you can pull the love train baby and you can repeat thank you Jesus
one reason Marvin loved his father was he offered him Jesus
Jesus left a long time ago said he would return kingdom to come
he left us a book to believe in we've got an awful lot to learn
Marvin says we'd better believe it Marvin says we've got a lot to learn
we've got to learn he is returned kingdom to come is kingdom come
this is the father's world this world won't die father's voice won't
we've got to learn it's too late to play dead in the low cars
Aretha sings "Wholly Holy" on her "Amazing Grace" album
Aretha makes up new words to go with Marvin's song as she goes along
moving and grooving with love doing and fooling with love
Southern California Community Choir behind her it's not doo it's who
it's not who it's *ooooooo—ooo—ooo—oooooo* so smooth and so zealous
if it could only be that night silent night across the nation.

Heartbeat rhythm of the bass heartbeat rhythm across this land
Marvin said if we stop if we listen to the rhythm of our heartbeat
Marvin said we'll hear the rhythm of the father's voice
the sound there before Motown sound of the voice before the bass
if we stop long enough we'll be gathered brought together by the voice
if we stop long enough we'll be laid by the voice that lays
da-*duh* da-*duh* da-*duh* da-*duh* da-*duh* da-*duh* da-*duh* da-*duh* da-*duh*
that the heart would be torn out da-*duh* da-*duh* da-*duh*
heartbeat rhythm Marvin said his church lived within his own heart
would be torn out da-*duh* da-*duh* da-*duh* da-*duh* da-*duh* da-*duh* da-*duh*
the way they did his life it makes him want to holler
Marvin thought they were the lawyers the lawyers from the government
Marvin thought cocaine was the boy who made slaves out of men
it's the word and child who fixed Marvin's mouth it's the father
it's the father who fixed Marvin's mouth his father in his heart
in the Chicago Museum of Science and Industry there's a model heart
model heart to walk in children held by their parents
what the children hear is da-*duh* da-*duh* da-*duh* *da-duh* da-*duh*
listening to Marvin what I hear is da-*duh* da-*duh* da-*duh* da-*duh* da-*duh*
listening to Marvin I want to cry it makes me want to cry
listening to Marvin I want to holler and throw up both my hands
like Edgar under the weight of this sad time this same sad time
I'm a witness I'm wandering not praying in the house of the voice
I'm wandering not grooving wandering moving on the wrong beat

Poem Beginning With A Line By Traherne

A tree apprehended is a tree in the mind
black locust with its bark put on in slabs
seams between the slabs ivy around them
the ivy around the trunk and further up
branches of the tree all their divarication
branches of the tree out over lawn and garden
myriad tiny leaves myriad tiny reflectors
leaves reflect leaves in parallel rows
the several parts of the tree extended in space
bark trunk branches tiny leaves extended
this extension is in the mind's apprehension
the mind's full with the parts of the tree
the mind is full and the air is pocked
the air this morning is pocked with emptiness.

The Rougher Black Music

*...the rougher black music: if someone had done that
once—maybe it would have been very great. But as it goes
on and on in every restaurant and every bar and—It becomes
something to escape from*

—George Oppen

It is very great music and something to escape from
as great as Mozart as great as the three boys
in Bergman's movie they sing from a balloon
they return the magic flute to the prince
they pray for heaven on earth for men like gods
greatness of the boys who sing with a serene solemnity
who sing the serene and solemn greatness of Mozart
as great as Mozart the rougher black music
black music which is neither serene nor solemn
black music which has made me dance against my will
twisted seized and twisted me *katechōntai te kai echōntai*
which has seized me and made me dance the twisted dance
which has seized me which has made me to fall down
black music which goes on and on seizing and twisting
I'm not a prince the three boys can't help me
where I live is no heavenly paradise men are not gods.

226

The Threefold Kiss

The father kisses those gathered together in three circles
some fall to their knees some wave their hands
and some are left wounded by the father
left cut and wounded by the father's honeyed tongue.

Reflexive

Consider whether you can be solitary and alone
whether you can sit alone like a sparrow
like a sparrow in an indentation in the ground
an indentation in the deep red ground
consider whether you can be like this in a valley
valley of vision where the ground is deep red
valley of vision where there are no roses
where there is not even a secret rose
consider whether you can remain in such a valley
in a valley of vision which is always the same
where the ground is always deep red ground
where there is not even a secret rose
consider whether you can remain like a sparrow
whether you can sit alone like a sparrow
like a sparrow in an indentation in the ground
in a valley of vision which is always the same.

Saul And David

King in the midst of the house king in space of the house

the king sits alone in the ghastly space of the house

the king sits alone in the dark in the midst of the house

no phosphorescent flower to light up the dark

hand of the king holds no phosphorescent flower

there is no flower and there can be no hope of rest

the king sits alone in the dark in the midst of the house

the king sits alone in the ghastly space of the house

king in the midst of the house king in space of the house.

Saul threw the spear once and David was nailed to the wall

spear of the king nailed the singer of the voice to the wall.

King in the midst of the house king in space of the house

the king sits alone in the ghastly space of the house

the king sits alone in the dark in the midst of the house

no phosphorescent flower to light up the dark

hand of the king holds no phosphorescent flower

the king sits alone in the dark in the midst of the house

the king sits alone in the ghastly space of the house

king in the midst of the house king in space of the house.

The Game With Red

How can a child immediately doubt what it is taught?
—Wittgenstein

Deepened by black red made deep by black
deepened and dark darker at the top
doorway without a door's always darker
deep red dark red always darker at the top.

What I can do is move wandering movement
what I can do is move in a wandering movement
wandering stumbling on the wrong beat
child in the dark with my eyes closed
child in the language game with red
who cannot win the game with red
what I cannot do is move outside the game
what I cannot do is get outside the doorway
the dark red doorway without a door
I cannot get outside the dark red doorway.

Speeded Up Played Faster

The slow the small steps are speeded up played faster
the teacher shows her pupil how to play faster
speeded up the slow the small here comes the bride steps
how to play faster teacher shows her pupil how
they make an intertwined trio with the keyboard
hand on her shoulder hand guiding her pupil's hand
intertwined hands their hands faster on the keyboard
how to play faster teacher shows her pupil how
speeded up the slow the small steps as in a dream
they make an intertwined trio completely free
they are free among lights in a dark wood
they are free among submerged lights glimmering off and on
how to play faster the teacher shows her pupil
speeded up all the steps of their composition
they make an intertwined trio with the keyboard
hand on her shoulder hand guiding her pupil's hand
intertwined hands their hands faster on the keyboard
speeded up how the teacher shows her pupil how.

At Arrowhead

Whether seeing after seeing is of any use
whether after-seeing can preserve shadows
the shadows of ferns their ambiguity
whether there can be shadows without invasion.

Whether this kind of seeing is of any use
whether the shadows can be preserved
shadows of what was howling wilderness
whether there can be shadows without invasion.

Whether long sought after seeing is of use
whether shadows should be preserved
shadows of mountains playing hide-and-seek
whether there can be shadows without invasion.

Whether this seeing was ever of any use
whether there should be preservation
shadows of clouds blackening the mountains
whether there can be shadows without invasion.

For Me

One last passionate pavan
yes one last passionate pavan
complete with a flow of my tears no less
for what I lack for me.

Not the dancing master's way
dancing master made out of words
tears wear away the contrived word-face
resignation word-face.

This one last slow dance saved for me
saved for me myself
saved for me by myself all by myself
myself without company.

Without any young soul rebels
not even my bones
poet torn in two and no swerving bones
poet torn by you know who.

I cry as I dance I'm moved to tears
this dancing moves me
Jackie Wilson: "lonely teardrops"
lonely teardrops for me.

SUN & MOON CLASSICS